BLOCKCHAIN
FOR THE
ENTERPRISE

MANAV GUPTA

For Sonia

CONTENTS

LIST OF FIGURES

LIST OF TABLES

FOREWORD

I first came to experiment with blockchain related technologies in 2013 when an IBM internal workgroup explored cryptocurrencies. The work stalled over other priorities and the general feeling was that cryptocurrencies were not applicable for enterprises. To be honest, I didn't get that far with the promise of blockchain.

Fast forward to 2015, and every CIO read the same article over the Thanksgiving period and there was tremendous fervor for this revolutionary technology called blockchain that would change everything we know and did. The Linux Foundation started the Hyperledger Project and there was tremendous interest generated worldwide. The passion of the participants in the meet-ups around the Toronto region I attended struck me. For the first time I saw business executives huddled with young people trying to grasp the technology. Soon a pattern emerged. The meet-ups would have Bitcoin fanatics, Ethereum and other cryptocurrency fans, and "others". The last category was most interesting—those that could feel the excitement, grappled with the technology, and tried to make sense beyond cryptocurrency.

As I learned the technology by engaging in proof of concepts and first projects, I realized how different and diverse its applications were. Soon the proof of concepts gave way to production deployments, and the fervor escalated for distributed ledger technologies almost as much for cryptocurrencies.

Over time, I became a speaker at these meet-ups besides a participant. The same set of questions being asked every single time struck me. It was as if people felt they could do something groundbreaking if only they could understand the technology. It didn't matter what industry they belonged to. Everyone wanted to do or be seen doing something with blockchain. And for that they needed to have at least a basic knowledge of the technology.

I wrote *"Blockchain for Dummies"* in 2017 to answer the most common questions, and separate blockchain from Bitcoin. The readers received the book well, but it spawned yet more questions.

The idea for a new book emerged. One that would be more ambitious. A book that would distill everything I knew about blockchain, and how to implement it within the enterprise. The idea consumed me. I couldn't sleep and just had to work on it. I sought collaborators within and outside IBM. The response was overwhelming and gave me the impetus to work. Alas, most of the contributors fell one by one to the usual culprits of business priorities, time constraints, and, lack of knowledge.

I too suffered. I expected to finish this project no later than December 2017 and spent many nights reading, re-reading, experimenting, and writing. It became a Sisyphean task since the technology was moving to that I had to rewrite chapters. The enthusiasm wore off and tiredness set in. I realized the enormity of the task and that with an evolving technology, there is no such thing as a perfect book.

So, what you have in your hand is my best effort at putting to paper all the topics I have come across when talking to enterprise clients about blockchain. I have selected topics for their relevance, timeliness, and applicability to enterprise use cases.

ACKNOWLEDGEMENT

This book stands on the shoulders of the giants both indirectly and directly. This work builds on Paul Baran's communication network design using 'redundancy' and 'digital' technology, Satoshi Nakamoto who developed bitcoin, authored the bitcoin white paper, created and deployed bitcoin's original implementation; Vitalik Buterin who co-founded Ethereum; the many people who developed and released ICOs; the Hyperledger project started by the Linux Foundation; and all enthusiasts who have forwarded the state of the art around distributed networks.

I am thankful to all contributors to this project. Aarsh Kak provided substantial content for the use of blockchain for social good. James Murphy from the IBM Watson IoT Platform team contributed to blockchain and IoT both in material and spirit. Nitin Gaur, Director IBM Blockchain Labs, provided initial guidance for the book, and contributed to blockchain in enterprise space. I am grateful to Dror Futter, Partner, Rimon Law and Practicing Law Institute (PLI) for contributing the material in legal issues around blockchain. I am indebted to the direct contribution of Stephane Mery, Distinguished Engineer & Chief Architect, IBM Operational Decision Manager, for the work on extending smart contracts in real world blockchain deployments. Kiran Vaidya, Product Manager at U.Cash, provided inputs on the section on overview of Ethereum.

There were several contributors who reviewed parts of the book as it evolved, and this work would have been a shadow of itself if it was not for their contributions. Luc Desrosiers, IBM Industry Platform Solution Architect, provided guidance, critique and inputs to the overall content and specific inputs to enterprise implications, and smart contracts. Ahmed Abbas, Executive Architect & Blockchain Practice Leader, IBM Egypt, provided excellent critique that expanded my thinking and improved the content accuracy in the areas of general book organization, implications of blockchain for the enterprise, and architectural guidance.

I want to thank my employer IBM, and the IBM Blockchain community at large for pushing the boundaries of the world's knowledge on blockchain by their engagements around the world. This book has benefitted by the many press releases, conferences, papers, and discussions I have had with IBMers around the world.

I would like to thank Brad DesAulniers, IBM Cloud Architect, for investing the time to push this project over the boundary, when I was struggling to see the finish line.

I want to thank my parents for pushing me to grow and expand my boundaries.

CHAPTER 1

INTRODUCTION

The democratization of high-speed Internet access along with advancements in peer-to-peer networking and cryptography have enabled the rise of the blockchain technology. The blockchain is a design pattern where each block contains a record of the transactions protected by cryptography, and it writes each block only after approval through a consensus mechanism. It writes the blocks onto the blockchain in chronological order to form a chain, with each block containing a hash of the previous block.

The backbone of the future peer-to-peer transaction network, blockchain technology provides an open and distributed cryptographic ledger shared across all nodes that take part in the network. The ledger records every performed transaction, and all participants in the network share the secured ledger. Ledgers are programmable, meaning actions it can take actions on a business transaction hitting the ledger.

In November 2008, a mysterious white paper appeared on the Internet, written under the pseudonym Satoshi Nakamoto, which described a new method for creating a distributed digital currency system by cryptographically chaining blocks of data together. The source code of Bitcoin implemented this concept, with its goal being to overcome the shortcomings of physical commodities such as currency. The rise of Bitcoin gave birth to the crypto-economy and brought the world's attention to the underlying blockchain technology.

1.1 Why all the fuss?

In any business network, there are multiple participants such as buyers, sellers, and regulators that have varying degrees of interest in tracking, accessing or interchanging an asset of value. Because these participants do not trust each other, they keep separate records of all transactions and then reconcile their ledgers to ensure that everyone's records reflect reality. This reconciliation is a costly operation that many industries have to maintain and support to comply with the regulatory authorities. Blockchain provides the ability to create business networks but takes away the centralized nature of business today and removes friction by replicating the data at every node on a distributed network to create permanence and resilience.

The reason blockchain technology is so disruptive is that it can solve the problem of authenticity without reliance on any trusted intermediaries, and independent instant verification, regardless of where the data originates from in the network.

Consider global trade finance – the financing of international trade flows essential for businesses to survive. A seller manufacturing goods in one country may require the buyer to pre-pay for goods to minimize the risk of non-payment upon delivery. The buyer may require the seller to document the shipment of goods before payment. Both the buyer and seller may engage banks in their countries to act as middlemen and mitigate risk. For example, the buyer's bank may provide a letter of credit to the seller's bank as a means of assurance of payment upon receipt of documentation such as bill of lading. The seller's bank may extend a loan to enable the seller to manufacture and ship the goods. According to the World Trade Organization, 80% to 90% of the world's trade transactions involve some kind of trade finance, by credit or guarantee to that credit. Global trade finance is a process of dizzying complexity and requires manual checks of authenticity, verification of legitimacy of the buyer and seller, and the high cost of this process restricts access to trade finance for smaller businesses. Using blockchain can enable digitization of real-time trade details and smart contracts can verify them. The buyer and seller can have access to the same information at the same time and reduce the costs of verification, reduce the time taken for reconciliation in case of disputes.

According to a McKinsey report, the global cross-border payments industry will generate $2.2 trillion in revenue by 2020. Any cross-border payment in the US takes 3 to 5 days for settlement, and costs an average of $42, and has an error-rate of 3% to 5%. With a distributed ledger on blockchain, the payments can happen in the same way as people share images, videos, and messages on peer-to-peer networks. The Internet of Value that blockchain enables allows users to share any asset of value including stocks, loyalty points, music, art, land titles, and more.

In the power industry, the value chain of transactions spans power generation, transmission, distribution, retail, and peer-to-peer transactions. Electricity changes hands several times between generation and consumption. Power relies on existing cumbersome trading and clearing systems to support complex markets, and blockchain provides a straightforward mechanism to encode units of power in smart contracts. The meter data can be fed onto the distributed ledger to modernize the wholesale electrical transaction processes and unlock new opportunities such as peer-to-peer energy trading where neighbors can sell excess power to each other.

Another interesting prospect of blockchain-based value transfer systems is the possibility of making tiny transactions, as tiny as a fraction of a penny, economically viable. Instead of creating click-baiting news headlines just to attract more views for the ad banners on the website, companies could be more accurately rewarded for creating insightful and meaningful content that the readers enjoy, irrespective of how many ad banners are shown and how many clicks the website generates. For example, it could utilize tiny, automated transactions as an e-mail spam filter that would be very difficult to circumvent. By setting a nano-scale price tag on sending an e-mail message, the cost would be insignificant to any normal use of e-mail, but it would grow to prohibitive proportions when trying to send millions of spam e-mails.

Industry leaders already recognize the power of Blockchain. Vitalik Buterin, founder of Ethereum says "While most technologies automate workers on the periphery doing menial tasks, blockchains automate away the center. Instead of putting the taxi driver out of a job, blockchain puts Uber out of a job and lets the taxi drivers work with the customer directly". Blythe Masters, CEO of Digital Asset Holdings says "The blockchain is the financial challenge of our time. It is going to change the way that our financial world operates". Ginni Rometty, Chairman & CEO of IBM has stated "Anything that you can conceive of as a supply chain, blockchain can vastly improve its efficiency. It doesn't matter if it's people, numbers, data, [or] money". According to Peter Thiel, co-founder of Paypal, "Bitcoin is the beginning of something great: a currency without a government, something necessary and imperative".

Several features of the blockchain technology have the potential to disrupt several industries in the long-run when leveraged in relevant use-cases.

- Blockchains replicate the distributed ledgers over a peer-to-peer network such that all participants have access to the same information, and the distributed network does not have a single point of failure. Thus no individual, organization, country or government has special privileges over other members. The ledger is transparent to all participants with no single points of failure.

- A blockchain network establishes trust by using consensus algorithms that determine the order and integrity of transaction information, without requiring a trusted intermediary. As a result, we are no longer dependent on a potential single point of a failure (such as a trusted intermediary).

- Once written on the blockchain, a block cannot be altered without altering all subsequent blocks. This built-in immutability provides an audit trail that is applicable across industries.

- Business automation via smart contracts: Blockchains provide a mechanism to encode the rules of operation as computer code on the blockchain along with transaction data. The contract code can execute on pre-determined conditions thus making transaction validation easier, cheaper, and more reliable.

Some implications of blockchain for enterprises are:

- **The redefinition of trust**: The trust protocols have evolved over human progress from the early barter systems to modern-day digital exchanges. With economic & societal progress, trust bearers evolved from tribal chiefs to central authorities like Tallies, to central & commercial banks. These institutions of centralized trust acted as bookkeepers, and governments issued money backed by precious metals such as gold to encourage trust in the monetary system. Over time this practice evolved to issuing fiat money without the backing of a physical commodity, giving the central banks an essential record-keeping function as the delegated trust bearers. Public trust in banks eroded over time due to lack of transparency, financial crises and subsequent bailouts, and hacking attacks on banks. Blockchain replaces the trust bearers of yesterday with a more robust, decentralized model over a distributed ledger shared among a network of computers. Real trust happens when multiple independent parties have their copy of transaction information, with no single authority to govern the process, and only parties involved in the transaction can see it and make alterations to it. As Leanne Kemp, Chief Executive Officer and Founder of Everledger said: "At its core, blockchain is shared ledger that allows participants in a business network to transact assets where everyone has control, but no one person is in control." Another way that blockchain helps build trust is the transparency of transactions, which establishes a traceable audit trail. "Blockchain will help pharmaceuticals keep up with the regulatory requirements," one Life Sciences CEO in India noted. The CEO of an Electronics company in Italy said: "Blockchain can bring transparency to the supply chain and make our image more trustworthy and reliable." Others expect traceability to improve processes and partner hand-offs. Smart contracts can encode the commitments between parties and help ensure compliance. Those smart contracts, a Government CIO from the U.S. said, could give them "the power to not only record property rights but enforce them."

- **The democratization of devices**: Blockchain allows Internet of Things (IoT) devices to gain greater autonomy by providing capabilities such as device identification, trusted transaction execution, and providing a complete record of transactions for audit. IoT devices can, therefore, become devices of transactions and economic value creation. For example, as soon as a product completes final assembly, it can be registered by the manufacturer in a supply chain blockchain network representing its beginning of life. After that, they can track each aspect of interaction with that device on the blockchain—from the sale, to repair, products revisions, recall notices, warranty notices, and eventual end-of-life. The devices can engage in complex transactions such as the use of smart contracts to barter power with one another or as a collective with the energy provider, check the provenance of adjacent parts, order supplies, run safety checklists—all without human intervention. For example, IBM developed with Samsung Electronics the Autonomous Decentralized Peer-to-Peer Telemetry (ADEPT) proof-of-concept, which demonstrated a Samsung washer autonomously reordering detergent, reordering service parts, negotiating power usage, and displaying advertising content. The blockchain technology will transform IoT into "Economy of Things" by not only enabling devices to autonomously engage in marketplaces but also supporting complex marketplace transactions.

- **Establishing automation economy**: Blockchains create excellent platforms for new ways of working. New ways to monetize and capitalize on things such as support for micropayments and skipping the intermediary fees, monetization of data itself, and giving rise to a sharing economy built around automation. In automotive insurance, rather than going straight to an insurer to get their vehicles covered, customers may now opt for a peer-to-peer style policy. Everything from factories to fleet could be shared, used, and capitalized on the blockchain. Hospitals are considering how they could share expensive equipment like a Magnetic Resonance Imaging (MRI) machines to mutual advantage. Blockchains, an Explorer CHRO in Healthcare from the U.S. observed, could "democratize the sharing economy by making it cheaper to create and operate a platform." Autonomously distributed markets could effectively distribute production resources between individual products and components in an ever-adjusting ad hoc basis, and smart contracts would ensure enforcement of business rules around transactions and regulations as agreed upon by the network participants.

- **Decentralized Autonomous Organizations**: The combination of smart contracts and cryptocurrency has enabled the rise of Digital Autonomous Organizations (DAOs) that operate as a system with no external human guidance, according to an incorruptible protocol specified in computer code and enforced on the blockchain. DAO's goal is to codify the rules and the decision-making apparatus of an organization, eliminating the need for documents and people in governing, creating a structure with decentralized control. Perhaps the most famous example is The DAO, conceived and programmed by the team behind German startup Slock.it, which is a company building "smart locks" that let people share their things (such as cars, boats, apartments) in a decentralized version of Airbnb. The DAO is the most successful crowdfunding project as of today (launched on 30th April 2016), raising over $150m from over 11,000 enthusiastic members. However, it also suffered an attack exploiting a recursive call bug that resulted in a loss of $50m value in post-theft valuations.

The full scope of the implications of this technology can take a while to understand but consider that all businesses today rely on central networks with trusted intermediaries in all aspects of our lives. We depend on trusted intermediaries that have become accepted mores, but we would be rid of them in a heartbeat if provided with the opportunity.

1.2 What is a cryptocurrency?

Traditional currencies (also known as "fiat" currencies) are a legal tender backed by the government that issues it. Organizations like central banks control the money supply and add counterfeit prevention measures to deter attackers. Law enforcement agencies are used to stop nefarious actors.

Cryptocurrency is a digital currency that uses encryption techniques to regulate the generation of currency units and peer-to-peer networking to prevent double spending, maintain accounts, balances, and transactions. Cryptocurrencies use advanced mathematical functions like cryptographic hash to raise the difficulty of attack and encode in a mathematical protocol the rules of creation of new units of the currency. Special entities in cryptocurrency networks called "miners" confirm transactions, after which the transactions are added to every node in the network. The miners are rewarded with a token of the cryptocurrency for confirming the transactions and maintaining the ledger.

1.3 Blockchain vs. Distributed Ledgers

The terms "blockchain" and "distributed ledger" are sometimes used interchangeably, but there is a subtle difference between the two.

A distributed ledger is a database that is spread across several nodes or computing devices. Each node replicates and saves an identical copy of the ledger.

The groundbreaking feature of distributed ledger technology is that the ledger is not maintained by any central authority. Updates to the ledger are independently constructed and recorded by each node. Once consensus has been reached, the distributed ledger updates itself and the latest, agreed-upon version of the ledger is saved on each node separately.

Blockchains are one form of distributed ledger technology. Not all distributed ledgers employ a chain of blocks to provide a secure and valid distributed consensus. Since it is a distributed ledger, it can exist without a centralized authority or server managing it, and its data quality can be maintained by database replication and computational trust. Data on a blockchain is grouped together and organized in blocks. Its append-only structure only allows data to be added to the database: altering or deleting previously entered data on earlier blocks is impossible. Blockchain technology is therefore well-suited for recording events, managing records, processing transactions, tracing assets, and voting.

1.4   Blockchain vs. Distributed Databases

Distributed database management systems (DDBMS) are collections of multiple, interrelated databases over a computer network. DDBMS use consensus mechanisms to ensure fault-tolerant communications and provide concurrency through locking and/or time-stamping mechanisms. Examples of DDBMS include NoSQL databases such as MongoDB and Riak.

Distributed ledgers are distributed databases that leverage cryptography and provide a decentralized concurrency control and maintain consensus about the existence and status of shared facts in trustless environments.

DDBMS are optimized for speed, not security. A distributed database is not optimal for entities that want to form a consortium of known participants but may not trust each other. A distributed database used as a "common consortium database" can run into problems—for example, if the server of an entity in a consortium is compromised, the whole system goes down since distributed databases are not designed to handle such scenarios.

In a consortium, one company will install and operate the database and will offer API access to other members. In this proven approach, one member becomes "more equal than others" because they host the database. Therefore, the host may have leverage over others, such as the ability to see information before others, having access to a more complete dataset, ability to restrict others, and so on.

Consortium members can create a new company to host the database, but it may be expensive. It does not motivate consortium members who do not host the database to contribute to its development because they feel they do not have complete access (since they only can use an API) and they feel it is just a product provided by the consortium leader. One may be using a distributed database, but it is still managed by a single company, which can shut it down, or fall victim to an attack.

Therefore, distributed databases may be more efficient, but have governance asymmetry, and may create a single point of failure.

The solution to this is to give each member of the consortium a copy of a database and implement an algorithm that synchronizes changes while also validating their authenticity. And this is "blockchain" or "distributed ledger technology."

The two main differences in distributed ledgers are:

- Decentralized control of the read/write access when compared to DDBMS.

- The ability to secure transactions in competing environments, without trusted intermediaries. The trust boundaries in a distributed ledger are redrawn to the organizational boundaries of each participant member of a consortium.

Figure 1.1 shows the relationship between blockchain, distributed ledgers, and cryptocurrencies.

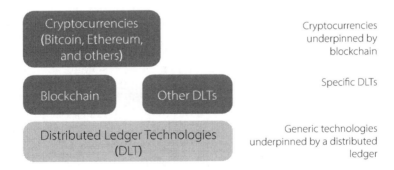

Figure 1.1: *Blockchain, distributed ledgers and cryptocurrencies*

1.5   How does an enterprise view blockchain?

In the enterprise context, blockchain is the technology to establish via radical openness, with no participant acting as a central authority. Enterprises must consider the meaning and impact of this radical openness. The manner in which the public blockchain operates is with relative simplicity by supporting a distributed master list of all (currency) transactions, which is a validated through a trust system supported by a consensus mechanism. However, an enterprise cannot apply this model of the trustless system without changing the fundamental tenets of the blockchain. For one, the exchange of computing power (or electricity) to achieve transaction finality is not appealing due to cost and scaling concerns. For example, Bitcoin has an average transaction commit time of 10 minutes, which will not be acceptable for most enterprise use cases. Bitcoin's capacity is around 200m transactions per year, but any midsize bank alone can exceed this limitation. Once blockchain tracks supply chain, provenance, data integrity, and identity, the number of transactions can explode. For example, many organizations must adhere to the Know Your Customer (KYC) process, which requires collection and verification of the identity of their clients. KYC records are updated periodically, and large organizations such as banks surpass the number of transactions to collect, verify, notarize the existence or authenticity of a record and its status. Once we factor in business logic, consumer protection, and privacy laws, the need for permission structures becomes obvious and makes public blockchains somewhat less appealing.

The blockchain influences enterprises in several ways:

- **Solves the fundamental problems of Time and Trust**: These two constructs apply to inefficiencies and costs in various industries such as some financial services, supply chain, logistics, and healthcare to name a few. *The Economist* dubbed blockchain "the trust machine," which allows "people who have no particular confidence in each other to collaborate without having to go through a neutral central author-ity." The lack of a central source of trust impacts system integrity in three ways—the problem of double-spending, establishing the trustwor-thiness of other participants in a decentralized network, and establish-ing transaction veracity. Blockchain solves these three problems via a consensus protocol that addresses the Byzantine's general problem, allowing all participants to possess a full copy of the ledger, and the use of cryptographic technologies for public and private keys used by participants to authenticate transactions. These three pillars of blockchain technology—decentralization, consensus, and cryptography, build the foundation for a tamper-proof ledger that enables trust without a central authority. Once trust has established, time benefits follow. For example, IBM Global Financing is the world's largest technology financier managing $44B in financial assets in 60 countries. With blockchain, they reduced the average dispute resolution time from 40+ days to less than 10 days, with a target of a few hours. Systemic trust binds the interaction between parties because the transactional record is stored as an immutable history on the blockchain—it is this characteristic that lends itself to non-repudiation and incentivizes fair play. This trust system leads to reduced risks and the applied technology constructs such as cryptography, encryption, smart contract, and consensus create quality gates that reduce risk and add security to the transaction system.

- **Reduce friction**: For centuries, global trade has been the single greatest creator of wealth in human history, and market friction is the most significant obstacle to wealth. Anything that adds inefficiencies or increases risk in business transactions is friction. Businesses have overcome many such frictions either by introducing institutions, instruments or technologies to reduce risk and achieve efficiencies. For example, digital signature technology solves the problem of impersonation and tampering in digital transactions. However, three frictions dominate—information, interaction, and innovation. Blockchain as the distributed ledger technology has the promise to eliminate all three. Blockchain eliminates information frictions caused by imperfect data, inaccessibility of data, and risks to data, since all participants have access to the same information, and use of encryption technologies provide safeguards against nefarious access. Smart contracts and distributed consensus eliminate interaction frictions of the cost of transaction verification or reliance on intermediaries. Blockchain promises to unlock innovation frictions by equipping enterprises to respond to digital disruption, provide a complete audit trail of transactions for regulatory purposes, and enabling established enterprises to be agile. According to CITI analysts, "Blockchain's main benefit is reducing friction. There are many third-party services that 'sell efficiency,' and we believe these businesses are the most at risk if Blockchain takes off and removes the friction these companies profit from." Another example is the use of digital money in developing markets as it removes customer friction and increases financial inclusion, such as the demonetization drive in India which has seen the rise of digital wallet providers.

- **Increase privacy**: In some blockchain implementations each item posted in the ledger is encrypted and permissions limit who can view the item. Members of a business network can only join upon granting of access by a Certificate Authority that provides both enrollment and transaction certificates. The network members can also sign each item put on to the ledger to identify who put the item on the ledger, creating greater visibility yet protecting privacy through the use of per-transaction certificates. Blockchains like Hyperledger may also provide encryption certificates to secure communication channels to off-chain systems.

- **Fuel disruptive innovation**: In the purest form, disruption is when a smaller company, focused on the lower and least profitable end of the market, rises towards a challenging competitor of incumbents in the profitable customer segments. For established enterprises, disruptive innovation occurs when it becomes necessary for companies to elaborate a strategy to manage a radical change in value creation. The business models for digital transformation have four dimensions to their strategy—use of technologies, changes in value creation, structural changes, and financial aspects. Blockchain affects the first two dimensions—since it is used to bypass intermediaries and reduce friction within systems. Thus, it has the potential to be disruptive. The World Economic Forum acknowledged blockchain as one of the top 10 emerging technologies in 2016. A 2016 Moody's report found that many companies are assessing how

13

the blockchain technology could affect their business and found that the technology had applications in sectors ranging from capital markets and trade finance, healthcare, and energy, to government taxation. The Chinese market is creating new business opportunities in areas such as trusted value exchange, digital asset management, and smart contract execution in unknown industry environments such as banking, insurance, internet finance, financial exchange services, retail, logistics, energy, and government. Frost & Sullivan estimated that the Automotive industry's spending on blockchain would reach 0.6% of its IT spend for functional areas such as mobility services, retailing, and leasing. The UK Government Office for Science published a recent report on the potential of the blockchain technology in governmental services, identifying use cases in protecting physical infrastructure, departments for work and pension, improvement of international aid systems, and potential in taxation. TenneT, the national electricity transmission system operator of Netherlands, is exploring the use of a permissioned blockchain network to integrate flexible capacity supplied by electric cars and household batteries into the electrical grid. These are brief examples of the vast potential of blockchain applications across industries.

The rest of this book provides a technical overview of blockchain from the enterprise, example use cases, criteria to select blockchain in solving business problems, blockchain technology roundup, and strategies for adoption of blockchain in enterprise.

CHAPTER 2

BLOCKCHAIN – A TECHNICAL OVERVIEW FOR THE ENTERPRISE

The sudden doubling in the price of Bitcoin in just two months in 2017, sparked a cryptocurrency gold rush. Bitcoin, Ethereum, and other alt-coins also soared giving them a collective market value of over $80 billion.

While the public, permissionless incarnations of blockchain technology may spark virtual tulip mania, the experiments with private, permissioned blockchains have also taken off. Sometimes the two have become cyclical, each riding the crest of other's wave. Cryptocurrencies of all types rely on the process of mining to unlock units of currency for transactions and online exchanges but may require gargantuan computing hardware setups working around the clock to beat other miners.

However, blockchain in the business context is different. The term 'distributed ledger technology' is being used to distance the term blockchain from Bitcoin.

In this chapter, I establish the business context and lay the groundwork for a deeper dive into the technology. I will start by defining blockchain for the enterprise, the changes it causes to basic business processes, benefits, hurdles, potential areas of disintermediation, and disruption.

2.1 Types of Blockchain technology

The blockchain technologies are of the following categories:

- **Public Blockchain**: A public blockchain is one anyone in the world can read and access. And anyone with a valid node can make transactions and check transaction validity. Any individual or organization can be a part of the process for determining addition of new blocks to the chain. Participants do not need permission from any authority to join the network. Participants are unknown to each other and trust emerges from game-theory incentives, which often involve spending physical resources such as computing power. Public blockchain are censorship resistant, may have reversals possible (contradictory to their original intent), and are suitable only for on-chain assets. Bitcoin, Ethereum, and Ripple are examples of public blockchain.

- **Private Blockchain**: If members know the identity of others in the network and can trust them to act honorably most of the time, there is no need to introduce artificial incentives to ensure co-operation. On an aggregate level, the lack of the need to spend physical resources makes the network much faster, more flexible and more important, much more efficient. Such blockchain networks have a central organization to assign permissions and the members may have varying levels of read and write access. Traditional security techniques may further secure private blockchain such as integration with Certificate Authority, and the use of public/private keys to enable fine grained privacy for the data written on the blockchain. Private blockchains are more attractive to business to recreate their existing networks or create new networks for fulfilling business requirements. Also known as Distributed Ledger Technology (DLT), private blockchains can host off-chain assets due to their authenticated, permissioned approach to validation. In this capability, permissioned blockchain has legally-accountable transaction validators, have settlement finality (no reversals) and are suitable for integrating with off-chain assets such as securities, fiat currency, and ownership titles. Examples of private blockchain are Hyperledger Fabric and Multichain.

- **Consortium Blockchain**: Consortium blockchains are where several entities within an industry vertical such as banking, healthcare, or utilities, come together to form an industry network, and are partly-private. Members of a consortium blockchain share the capabilities of private blockchains, providing greater decentralization yet provide the same benefits affiliated with private blockchain such as transaction privacy and efficiency. One aim of consortium blockchains is encouraging organizations in that industry to come together for technology trials, shared investments, and enablement of new services. Examples of consortium are R3, Corda, and B3i.

2.2 Blockchain System Concepts

Blockchain can serve as a distributed ledger technology where paricipants' identity is known. Such a ledger may record a wide range of items, such as asset ownership, asset transfer transactions, and contract agreements. Some participants may exhibit byzantine behavior but most act with honesty, enabling the network to achieve consensus with relative efficiency and expediency. The nodes are computers of the participants, each with a local copy of the ledger containing a full record of all transactions.

Each new transaction updates the ledger. However, instead of an overwriting an old record that denotes a transaction, a new entry is added into the ledger and the blockchain protocol shares transaction information with all nodes using a peer-to-peer protocol. This ensures each of the nodes maintains a database of all historical, valid transactions.

It groups transactions into blocks, and each block references the previous block of transactions achieving a temporal ordering of transactions. The network selects a leader node at random, and determines the specific order of transactions based on the consensus algorithm.

It uses complex data structures such as Merkle trees to store all transactions in a way that any change to a historical transaction in a single node results in invalidate states if one node would recalculate the current state from all historical transactions.

The blockchain network ignores any transactions considered invalid by other nodes in the network, and various forms of throttling or penalties to nodes that propose invalid transactions consistently.

Most blockchain implementations have support for a scripting code to execute business logic triggered by a transaction called *smart contracts*.

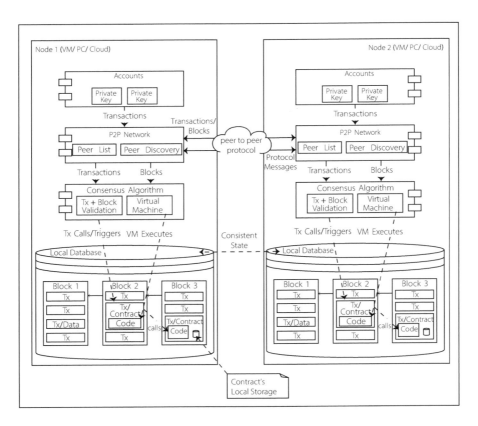

Figure 2.1: *Blockchain component diagram*

2.3   Updates to distributed ledger

When there is no central trusted party, the process of updating the ledger relies on a process of achieving consensus among the nodes for all new information added to the ledger. There are two parts to achieve consensus:

- **Validation**—The nodes taking part in the transaction validate that every transaction in the new candidate block for addition to the blockchain is legitimate. The blockchain network may also nominate one or more nodes not taking part in the transaction to validate the block contents.

- **Broadcast & Consensus**—This process enables the validating nodes to reach a consistent view of the new entry in the distributed ledger and broadcast the information about the new block to all other nodes.

2.4   What is blockchain in business?

Businesses don't exist in isolation. They exist in a network connected to customers, suppliers, and partners, and operate across geographic & regulatory boundaries in a logical business network. This business network is not static over time and will morph upon business acquisitions & mergers, introducing new products and services (which may create new consumers and suppliers), and technological changes. This interchange of goods and services across a business network creates a market. Global trade across a business network has generated wealth for centuries, measured as the sum of flow of goods and services across a business network. If business networks are fragment or inefficient, they constrain the growth of wealth. As Adam Smith noted, 'market friction is the ability of capital, labor, and technology to move forward to create economic success.'

The market created by a business network can be open (for example, fruit market, or an open-outcry commodities market) or closed (business supply chain financing, or bond market).

Interactions between parties in a business network create transactions, which record the exchange of an asset. Anything capable of being owned or controlled to produce value and has a positive economic value is an asset. Further, assets may be tangible (such as a house) or intangible (a mortgage on the house).

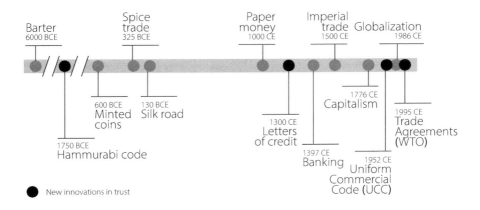

Figure 2.2: *Evolution of trust in business*

Technology innovations have helped overcome distance and address ineffi- ciencies in the era of modern capitalism. Introducing the Telegraph in 1837 had a direct impact on businesses, starting with the railways and expanding to the transport of goods and materials. Faster transports such as steamships and railways moved goods faster and cheaper. The subsequent introduction of telephony in 1876 developed city centers, office buildings and the concept of an urban worker society.

Throughout this technological advancement, one thing remained constant— the use of double entry bookkeeping in a principal book, known as a ledger. The invention by Luca Pacioli, a Franciscan friar in late 1400s, has remained in use today. A Ledger is THE system of record for a business and records asset transfer between participants that affect the business. Businesses today will have multiple ledgers for multiple business networks in which they take part. The ledger records all transactions, and the basic concepts have remained unchanged since its invention.

Today's asset transfer process can be inefficient, expensive and vulnerable since each party on the network maintains its ledger. Information sharing is at a minimum, and while the parties may engage in transactions, they use middlemen (such as banks, or regulatory bodies) to establish trust. The middlemen may view portions of each party's ledger to ensure regulatory compliance.

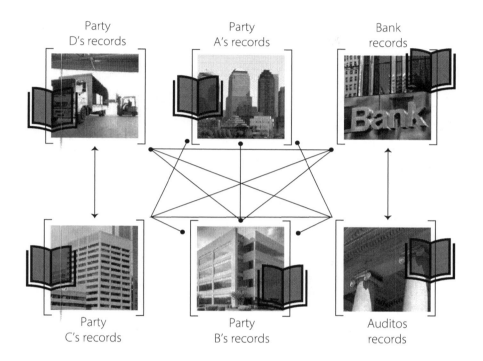

Figure 2.3: *Status quo of local ledgers maintained by each business participant*

Permissioned blockchain technologies share a ledger across the business network. The network will be closed (accessible only by the parties concerned), private (so only allowed participants can join), and requires permissions (to ensure that participants only see what they may view).

The business network participants will be the same - disintermediation is not a natural consequence of blockchain usage. The shared ledger is resistant to failures since it is replicated & distributed. There will be a consensus across the network where the provenance of information is clear and transparent. Transactions will be immutable (unchangeable) and final.

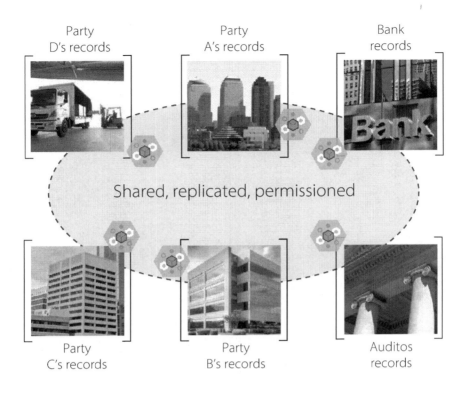

Figure 2.4: *Shared, permissioned ledger with blockchain*

It is this shared, replicated ledger that provides trust "digitally" by providing a mechanism for the participants in the network to arrive at a consensus, and usage of cryptographic algorithms to achieve the immutability of transactions (or 'records') once written on to the blockchain. Blockchain shifts the paradigm from information held by a single owner to the life history of an asset or transaction. Instead of messaging-based communications, the new paradigm is state-based: Information that was once obscure now becomes transparent.

The characteristics of blockchain for business are:

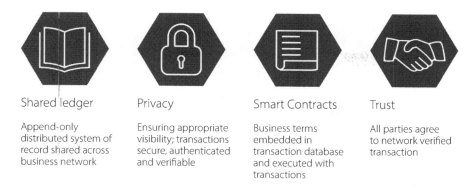

Shared ledger	Privacy	Smart Contracts	Trust
Append-only distributed system of record shared across business network	Ensuring appropriate visibility; transactions secure, authenticated and verifiable	Business terms embedded in transaction database and executed with transactions	All parties agree to network verified transaction

Figure 2.5: *Characteristics of an industrial blockchain*

2.5   Blockchain for business

- **Shared Ledger**: The shared ledger records all transactions across the business network. It is the is the system of record, the single source of truth. All participants in the network share the same copy of the ledger through replication over a peer-to-peer network. The ledger is permissioned, so participants see only those transactions they're allowed to view. Participants have identities which link them to transactions on the ledger, but they can select which aspects of transaction information other participants can view. Most modern databases store the world state of the data and keep the logs of transactions with the database as a separate "thing." Blockchain clients build the world state of the data from the blocks of authenticated transactions that are "chained" together. Thus, it is always possible to tell if something is valid, as it must have come from a validated history, and everyone agrees on the sequence of historical records.

- **Privacy**: With a permissioned blockchain, each participant has a unique identity, which enables the use of policies to constrain network participation and access to transaction details. Organizations can comply with data protection regulations by restricting access to known participants. Permissioned blockchains may allow participants to see only certain transactions, while they may give other participants, such as auditors access to a broader range of transactions. For example, if the Party A transfers an asset to Party B, both Party A and Party B can see the details of the transaction. Party C can see that A and B have transacted but cannot view the details of the asset transfer. If an auditor or regulator joins the network, privacy services can ensure that they see full details of all transactions on the blockchain network. Cryptographic technology — this time through the use of digital certificates — makes this possible. Just like a passport, a digital certificate provides identifying information, is forgery-resistant, and is verifiable. The blockchain network will include a certification authority who issues the digital certificate.

- **Trust**: The ledger is a trusted source of information. The most common mechanism used to establish trust is the use of a consensus algorithm by which a majority of the network members agree on the value of a piece of data or a proposed transaction, which then updates the ledger. Consensus algorithms allow the machines connected in a business network to work together as a group that can survive even if some members fail. Permissionless blockchain networks need cryptographic consensus to support participant anonymity and establish trust, such as the use of 'Proof Of Work' in Bitcoin. PoW is expensive and adds cost to preserve anonymity. However, in permissioned blockchain networks where the identity of the participants is known, other mechanisms can achieve network consensus. They use non resource-intensive consensus algorithms, ledger immutability, permissions, and a full audit trail of all assets to establish trust.

- **Smart Contracts**: A smart contract is a computerized protocol that executes the terms of the business contract. Smart contracts enable encoding in computer code contractual clauses (such as collateral, bonding, and delineation of property rights) to enforce compliance of contractual terms for a successful transaction. For example, a smart contract embedded in the operating system of the car may make the car inoperable unless the user completes the proper challenge-response protocol to verify rightful ownership. Smart contracts ensure a party in a business transaction that the counterparty will fulfill the promise with certainty and reduce costs for verification and enforcement. Smart contracts in the enterprise world are smart contract code accompanied by the traditional legal contract. For example, a smart contract code on a land registry blockchain for transferring the ownership of a house may update the land registry records in real time, and all participants (such as the city, realtors, lawyers, and banks) can view the sale when it happens. However, the homebuyer will insist on the traditional, legal contract with indemnity clauses to cover any undiscovered liens. Smart contracts have many potential applications and are fueling device democracy, such as the smart washer dryer that IBM and Samsung demonstrated at CES in 2015. These transactions still require a minimum level of trust to be viable but are ill-suited for legal contracts, which are expensive and involve legal entities.

2.6   How does the blockchain work?

Each participant in the business network hosts the blockchain network on their server (whether a physical server, a virtual machine or a Docker container running on their premises or in a cloud computing environment). The nodes representing the network participants connect to one another establishing a peer-to-peer business network.

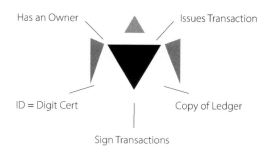

1. IT ALL STARTS WITH ONE NODE

Each node has an owner, maintains a local copy of the ledger, has a digital certificate that holds permissions for that node to join the business network and enables the node to issue transactions.

A blockchain is a continuously growing list of data records organized into a series of blocks. Each block contains a batch of transactions. Each block has a timestamp and a reference to the previous block.

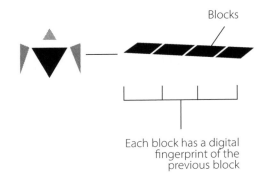

Blocks

Each block has a digital fingerprint of the previous block

2. EACH NODE HAS A SHARED LEDGER

Transactions include information about the asset transfer, the identity of the involved parties, and metadata such as transaction time, asset value, and contractual clauses.

Blockchain uses one-way cryptographic hashing to guarantee the integrity of data, encryption to guarantee data confidentiality, and digital signatures to ensure the authenticity of the sender of transaction data.

The nodes form a peer-to-peer network.

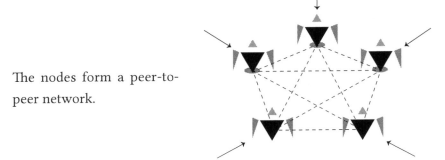

3. NODES FORM A PEER NETWORK

The users of the blockchain submit a transaction (via their node). A user signs the transaction with their digital signature (i.e., 'private key') and includes the address of the receiver (i.e., receiver's 'public key').

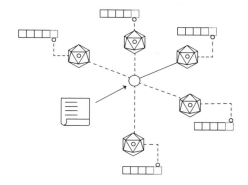

4. Users submit transactions

A block has one or more transactions. Before adding a block to the chain, the ledger network validates it through an iterative process that requires consensus from a majority of the members. The network may elect one or more nodes as consensus leaders, which ensure that they follow the network

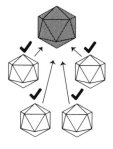

5. Consensus and leader election

rules. The network arrives at consensus through different methods (such as, 'proof of work' or 'proof of stake')

The blockchain technology codifies network rules as 'smart contracts'. After validating all the transactions in a block, it executes the transactions, and broadcasts the updated state of the ledger to the network. All nodes update their local copies to reflect the change of state.

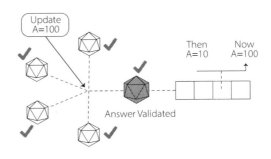

6. EXECUTION & RECOVERY

As the blockchain maintains the history of all transactions, it grows with transactions.

2.7   Business benefits of blockchain

- **Removes cost**: Business networks exist to facilitate the exchange of assets between buyers and sellers in a business transaction, who have to verify key attributes of any transaction before execution, increasing the need for intermediation as markets scale in size and geographic reach. The intermediaries or reputation systems in business networks perform this validation, forcing additional disclosures (such as those mandated by regulation). These mechanisms introduce a cost for verifying the attributes of a transaction. Further, there may be asymmetric information between the seller and the buyer (for example, the inability of the buyer to assess the quality or provenance of goods). However, transaction verification is costless with distributed ledger technologies and opens new types of transactions, intermediation and business models.

  A transaction inherits essential attributes upon initiation, such as the time of creation, information about the seller and buyer involved in it (i.e., where do the inputs come from, and where to deliver the outputs). Users rely on these attributes to perform related actions (e.g., the seller may ship the goods once the buyer transfers funds). Some of these actions take place for every transaction (e.g., settlement), while future events may trigger other actions. An interesting subset of future events is those that require additional verification. For example, a problem with the transaction may emerge, and original attributes may require re-verification via an audit. The audit is often costly as it may require a third-parties to mediate between buyer and seller.

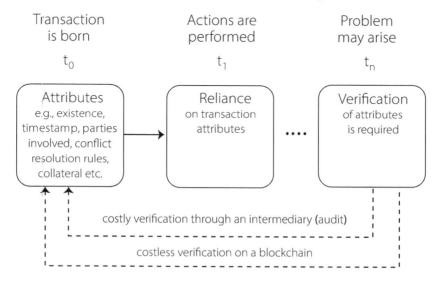

Figure 2.6: *Transaction verification on blockchain*

Blockchain technology changes this flow by allowing for costless verification of all the attributes when a problem emerges since it stores all transaction attributes (e.g., the time-stamp of a transaction, digital "fingerprints" of the individuals, goods or services involved). Blockchain technology may even deliver 'sousveillance'—an audit embedded in the marketplace itself.

- **Saves time**: The use of distributed ledger technology saves time in multiple ways. Smart contracts which codify business policies for routine and ad hoc checks of the stored transactions and associated asset ownership information save time. Most banks perform Know Your Customer

(KYC) checks out of centralized databases, and different departments within a bank will perform repeated checks of a customer. With blockchain, these checks are completed only once, and all departments can share the KYC status without breaking down the regulatory boundaries. IBM's Global Financing blockchain implementation has seen dispute resolution time reduced from 40+ days down to less than 10 days. Blockchain may some existing business processes redundant. For example, financial institutions could track the underlying structure and performance of mortgage-backed security on blockchain and make it accessible to relevant parties in real-time. Regulatory authorities could audit accounting records while preserving the privacy of the entities.

- **Increases trust**: For almost any supply chain—be it food, medical records, precious gems and minerals, real estate or credit default swaps, to name a few—success depends on the promise of transparency and auditability for all participants. The distributed ledger technology with the clever use of cryptography- and permission-based access ensures all participants have a single source of truth updated with each transaction, every time. Transaction metadata improves auditability and increases traceability.

- **Reduces risk**: Using distributed ledgers for settlement and reconciliation among network participants creates a more open and secure platform. Using a permission authority, public-key cryptography, and hashing algorithms reduces the risks of nefarious actors, double-spending, and malicious impersonation. Some blockchains may provide multiple mechanisms to enhance privacy (e.g., use of a per-transaction certificate), and sensitive information could be stored off-chain in a private database which is linked immutably to the blockchain entry using cryptography.

2.8   Example use cases

There is plenty of literature on the Internet that describes the uses of blockchain. Moody's Investor report on blockchain identified 25 use cases across a wide variety of industries such as financial institutions, healthcare, real estate, media, energy, and governments. Financial institutions have been developing blockchain-based solutions (e.g., payments, post-trade life cycle in capital markets, and trade finance) to gain cost efficiencies in times of constrained bank profitability. Blockchain startup Ripple is developing enterprise blockchain solutions for international payments, with its custom payment protocol and exchange network, and its cryptocurrency XRP.

Guardtime is an Estonian startup which uses blockchain enables to ensure the integrity of enterprise networks, prevent loss of critical digital assets and track data securely throughout the supply chain. The Holbertson School, a California-based software skills program, announced it would use blockchain technology to authenticate academic certificates to ensure that students claiming they passed courses at the Holbertson School aren't using accreditation they didn't earn. Visa and DocuSign unveiled a partnership in 2015 that used blockchain to build a proof-of-concept for streamlining car leasing, and making it into a "click, sign, and drive" process. Startups such as PeerTracks and Ujo Music have emerged, who aim to use smart contracts to let artists sell directly to fans without going through a record label, track rights owners, and automates royalty payments using smart contracts and cryptocurrency, respectively.

The figure 2.7 provides some of the use cases across several industries.

Cross Industry					
Shared reference data	FINANCIAL	GOVERNMENT	HEALTHCARE	INSURANCE	MANUFACTURING
Internal financial ledger	Letter-of-Credit	Land Registry	Medical records	Claims processing	Supply chain
Audit and compliance enablement	Cross currency payments	Vehicle Registry	Medicine supply chain	IoT integration for policy monitoring	Product parts
Regulatory view					
Improved efficiencies	Mortgages	Citizen ID			Maintenance tracking
Innovation					

Figure 2.7: *Blockchain use across several industries*

Table 2.1 summarizes technological cases with applicability across industries.

Table 2.1: *Technological cases across industries*

Use case area	Description	How it can be implemented on blockchain?	Benefits
Consensus	Competitors or collaborators in a business network may need to share some reference data. For example, banks may need to share bank routing codes; mining companies may need to share standards for part numbers for heavy machinery, etc. Each member maintains its reference data (such as routing codes), and forwards changes to the central authority for collection and distribution.	Each participant maintains its codes within a blockchain network. Blockchain allows a single view of the entire dataset so all participants can have access to the most updated information in the business network.	1. Consolidated, consistent dataset reduces errors. 2. Near real-time view of reference data which can reduce transaction verification time (for example, when part numbers for new types of drills). 3. Participants can to edit their own information subset to notify of changes to other participants
Immutability	Large organizations have data silos dispersed across many divisions and geographies. In some industries, regulatory rules may enforce data privacy rules which prohibit data sharing without traceability.	Distributed ledger can build a single source of truth from diverse data silos. Append-only and tamperproof qualities create high confidence financial audit trail. Privacy features in the blockchain network ensure data is accessible to allowed users only. Smart contracts enforce full traceability of access.	1. Lower cost of audit and regulatory compliance. 2. Provides 'seek and find' access to auditors and regulators. 3. Enables active compliance with full traceability baked into the blockchain network.

Audit and compliance need an indelible record of all transactions over a specified period. For example, the billing and marketing departments in a telecom company may share Call Detail Records, and law enforcement agencies may also require it in criminal inquiries.

Regulators and auditors can have read-only permissions to the entire shared-ledger, giving them a view on the system-of-record.

1. Near costless verification and compliance.

2. Proactively enforced compliance via smart contracts.

Compliance

A study of multinational organizations completed in 2011 estimated the average cost of compliance at $3.5million, and the average cost of non-compliance related issues at $9.4million. The most important compliance efforts are with external laws and regulation, for example:

- PCI DSS
- US state laws for data breach
- European Union Privacy Directive
- Sarbanes-Oxley

CHAPTER 3

MARKET AND INDUSTRY OVERVIEW

The hype around blockchain continues to build, and the disruptive potential is real as evidenced by the client applications cited in the book. Several market analysts estimate the blockchain market size to grow at a Compound Annual Growth Rate (CAGR) of 40.9% to 61.5% according to various analysts. Organizations are looking at blockchain for near costless transaction verification, transparency & immutability, and lower risk in business transactions.

3.1 Evolution

The blockchain market has continued to evolve in the areas of technology and business applications.

- Adam back invented the Hashcash Proof-of-Work function in 1997.

- In 1998, Nick Szabo introduced 'bit gold' as a mechanism for decentralized digital currency and smart contracts. A precursor to Bitcoin, it described a system for the decentralized creation of unforgeable proof of work chains, with each one being attributed to its discoverer's public key, using timestamps and digital signatures.

- In 2000 Stefan Konst published a general theory for cryptographically secured chains and suggested a set of solutions for implementation.

- Satoshi Nakamoto then conceptualized the first blockchain in 2008 and implemented the following year as a core component of the digital currency Bitcoin where it serves as the public ledger for all transactions.

- The first transaction in Bitcoin happened in block #170, which paved the way for the first real-world transaction. On 22 May 2010, Laszlo Hanyecz made the first real-world transaction by buying two pizzas in Jacksonville, Florida for 10,000 BTC.

- By 2014, "Blockchain 2.0" was a term referring to new applications of the distributed blockchain database. The Economist described one implementation of this second-generation programmable blockchain as coming with "a programming language that allows users to write more sophisticated smart contracts, thus creating invoices that pay themselves when a shipment arrives or share certificates which automatically send their owners dividends if profits reach a certain level." Blockchain 2.0 technologies go beyond transactions and "exchange of value without powerful intermediaries acting as arbiters of money and information."

3.2 Market Opportunity

The addressable blockchain market revenue opportunity is $2.5B in 2018, growing to $15B by 2021, according to MD&I Trend Analysis. The bulk of the market will be addressable in the form of Services given that custom, services-driven projects will drive the market in the early years.

1. The biggest blockchain market is the Financial Services industry which has already adopted blockchain solutions in clearing, and near-real-time securities settlement, cross-border remittances, and equity swap. The investment will grow even more in new application areas in 2017 including more back-office operations such as regulatory reporting, and KYC (Know Your Customer) processes. Several analysts forecast the blockchain market of $67.2M in 2016 to grow at a CAGR of 56% through 2021.

2. Analysts expect fastest adoption in the Healthcare/Life Sciences industries in 2017 in use cases such as clinical trial records, regulatory compliance, and medical/health records. They forecast the blockchain market $33.5 million to grow at a CAGRs of 66.5% through 2021.

3. Government & Retail industries have strong use cases and increasing adoption. The benefits of blockchain solutions of transparency and immutability make it very appealing for Government use cases including digital voting and reducing fraud (such as in social services) through smart contracts and the Retail use-case of secure transactions. Other industries are growing blockchain adoption, including Media and Energy.

3.3 Top blockchain trends

1. **Proofs-of-concept will slowly move to production**: There will be an increase in initiatives moving into production. Less than 5% of blockchain proofs-of-concept moving forward into production but this number will rise to double digits in the next 2 to 3 years as the technology matures and more skilled professionals are available.

2. **More traditional players and financial institutions will get involved in cryptocurrency**: In the next few years, at least one Tier 1 bank will offer cryptocurrency services and Initial Coin Offerings (ICOs). Consumers expect digital money that cryptocurrencies provide is connected to the Internet and unconstrained by geography or institutions. With the rise of digital wallets and technologies like Apple Pay, people expect that transactions should be free and that foreign exchange should be immediate. These are factors that the financial institutions will consider in offering new services around cryptocurrencies.

3. **Blockchain ecosystems will become critical success factors**: Memberships in consortiums and industry collaborations will increase. Business partners will align to ecosystems with easy-to-use APIs/tools, marketing support, and a clear revenue sharing model.

3.4 Growth Drivers for Blockchain

The survival of any organization depends on its ability to outperform competitors and marketplaces in attracting and rewarding talent, ideas, and capital. The pace of innovation has sped up as the transaction costs have plummeted with the rise of the Internet, leading to new platforms, business models and delivery of services and goods at unimaginable speeds. Startups take advantage of the changes in the underlying technology and lack of encumbrances by existing revenue streams (and associated costs and inertia) to challenge established businesses forcing them into foreclosure or rethinking of existing value chains.

As the world moves to overcome the hype surrounding blockchain, financial markets institutions are among the first to leverage the decentralized blockchain platform to define their futures. According to an IBM Institute of Business Value study, 14% of the financial markets institutions surveyed planned to go into blockchain production at scale in 2017, focused on payment clearing and settlement, wholesale payments, equity and debt issuance, and reference data. According to Accenture, the 'tipping point' will happen in 2018 when the early majority of financial services see the benefits of early adopters and new models emerge.

The significant factors in enterprise adoption of blockchain technologies are:

1. **Loss of faith in existing financial systems**: For the world's financial systems to function, it is essential that the general population has faith in it. The earliest remnant of paper currency called 'feiqian' ('flying cash') as the Chinese called it during the Ming dynasty, declared their circulation to last forever, and that 'to counterfeit is death'—extreme measures to introduce confidence in using paper currency instead of gold or silver. Fast forward to 2008 when the collapse of Lehmann Brothers had an enormous impact on the financial markets and erosion of trust—both system trust of citizens' in their institutions, and the validity of the underlying principles. The resulting financial crisis and subsequent disclosures of wrongdoings from some of the world's premier financial institutions further eroded trust. The U.S. Securities and Exchange

Commission has charged over 200 entities and individuals with total penalties exceeding $3.76 billion. According to the Edelman Trust Barometer conducted in January 2009, for instance, 65% of all respondents (a figure that rises to 84% in France) agreed that their government should impose stricter regulations and greater control over businesses in all industries. A survey by the non-profit National Association of Retirement Plan Participants found that only 13% of 5000 respondents had faith in their financial institutions in 2015. The Chicago Booth / Kellogg School's Financial Trust Index shows only 27.13% of Americans trust the nation's financial system. This erosion of trust led to the rise of anti-capitalist and anti-globalization sentiments around the world, and a desire to eliminate existing intermediaries. Bitcoin gained mainstream attention in 2011 with Silk Road but before mining became profitable, there were thousands of people dedicating resources and efforts to the currency. Any visit to a Bitcoin discussion forum provides evidence that an important core of the BTC community comprises libertarians who want to see the end of all fiat currencies. Curiosity, profit and politics motivated the initial adopters of Bitcoin although there is evidence that the initial interest was also the ability to deal in illegal activities. Regardless, Bitcoin paved way to a host of cryptocurrencies where developers have forked the original Bitcoin codebase and created their own version known as altcoins. The current market capitalization of altcoins exceeds $58 billion.

2. **Change in consumer behavior**: Everyday consumers want access to quick, convenient, and widely accepted payment methods. The two other waves of technological disruption happening with blockchain are the rise of social networks, and enterprise adoption of mobile technologies. 62% of US adults get their news on social media, e-commerce accounted for 11.7% of total retail sales in 2016, and mobile phones surpassed desktop and laptop computers in 2016. The rise of cryptocurrencies forced most countries to adopt initiatives for banks to do faster payments. The UK has Faster Payments, the Eurozone has SEPA, and the Chase introduced

ClearXchange in the US. Companies had to adopt creative branding and social media strategies since millennials trust their peers over advertisements (which had a stronger impact with baby boomers). A recent FICO report showed that millennials are five times more likely than those over the age of 50 to close all accounts with their primary bank, have no patience for the traditional fees imposed by intermediaries (like ATM withdrawal fee) and are more likely to interact with a financial institution via an app rather than walk into a branch. Cutting edge Fintech startups and new market entrants have capitalized on these technological and consumer behavioral changes, causing disruption to the traditional value chain of financial institutions. The Fintech startups have focused on four primary areas—payments, personal finance management, lending and investments. Global venture investment in Fintech grew to $17.4 billion in 2016 according to PitchBook. 'This signals Silicon Valley is coming. There are hundreds of startups with a lot of brains and money working on various alternatives to traditional banking', according to Jamie Dimon, CEO of Chase. Francisco Gonzalez, Chairman and CEO of BBVA said 'Up to half of the world's banks will disappear through the cracks opened by digital disruption of the industry'. Fintech is democratizing the playing field, providing targeted solutions to a smartphone happy consumer who is less willing to walk into a bank account, and using technologies like blockchain for faster transaction times. People are becoming less reliant on banks and instead using apps to fulfill services offered by banks. For example, TransferWise or Xoom to send money, filing taxes with SimpleTax, and managing outstanding payments on Satago.

3. **Venture capitalist investment**: Over 3 million people are estimated to be actively cryptocurrency like Bitcoin. The number of unique cryptocurrency wallets is estimated to be between 2.9 million and 5.8 million. This user adoption has also resulted in a direct impact on venture capital investment. According to an August 2016 report by the World Economic Forum (WEF), "The Future of Financial Infrastructure," over $1.4 billion

has been invested in the blockchain technology in just three short years. Over 90 corporations have signed on to blockchain development consortia, with at least 24 countries now investing in blockchain research and development. The WEF predicts that by 2017, 80 percent of banks will engage in projects implementing blockchain technology. Financial institutions have taken part to the tune of $320 million—for example, Goldman Sachs invested in the $50 million investment round of peer-to-peer payment startup Circle; Nasdaq, Visa and Citi invested $30 million in Chain.com, and NYSE, BBVA invested $75 million in Coinbase. The increased investment from venture capitalists and the rise of blockchain consortiums has led to an increased adoption of the blockchain technology for enterprises. For example, Hyperledger experienced a 30% QoQ member growth in Q4 2016 passing 100-member milestone, R3 gained five new members and completed a KYC trial with ten banks. Proof-of-Concept activity continued to increase throughout 2016 with over 50 PoCs announced in Q4 2016 with over 120 unique participants. Major technology providers introduced blockchain services to capture the market and mindshare. Microsoft launched its Blockchain-as-a-Service (BaaS) for Microsoft Azure to help organizations develop, test and deploy blockchain applications. IBM introduced a blockchain service on its Bluemix Cloud based on Hyperledger, enabling developers to test blockchain technology and use in production via its High-Security Business Network service. Partnerships and collaborations continued to grow in the blockchain technology market. Microsoft announced a collaboration with ConsenSys and Blockstack to create an open source, self-sovereign, blockchain-based identity system that allows people, products, apps and services to interoperate across blockchains, cloud providers and organizations. Deloitte partnered with BlockCypher, Bloq, ConsenSys, Loyyal, and Stellar, to provide new technological capabilities to its global financial institution client base. Ripple added Standard Chartered, National Australia Bank (NAB), Mizuho Financial Group (MHFG), BMO Financial Group, Siam Commercial Bank (SCB) and Shanghai Huarui Bank to improve their cross-border payments using blockchain.

4. **Growing recognition of broader potential**: Contracts, transactions, and the records of them are among the defining structures of our economic, legal, and political systems. With blockchain, we can imagine a world where contracts are code on the blockchain, and governed by the rules of the network and protected from deletion, tampering, and revision. In this world, every agreement, process, task, and every payment has a digital record and a signature that authorized network members can identify, validate, store and share. A recent report from Mckinsey & Company identified multiple, cross-industry use case categories that such as management of asset ownership & chain of custody, secure storage, confirmation, and distribution of identity-related information, exchange of assets on the blockchain, efficient payment transfers with lower friction and improved record keeping, and the use of blockchain to store information and access dynamic information. Blockchain will have the same foundational impact to digital transactions that TCP/IP did to the internet—unlocking of new economic value by lowering the cost of transactions. However, it is also clear that the proof-of-work method used by Bitcoin (and built people's trust in the blockchain 1.0 world) is unsustainable. The energy consumption estimates for the Bitcoin network range from 334 MW per year to 774 MW per year, sufficient to power 268,000 to 627,100 American homes. As the value of Bitcoin increases, the competition for mining new Bitcoin increases, driving up the computation complexity and the associated electricity. This model is unsustainable in the long run. The World Economic Forum has argued that blockchain is a new global resource to record anything of value to humankind. Paul Brody, principal and global innovation leader of blockchain technology at Ernst & Young, thinks all our appliances should donate their processing power to the upkeep of a blockchain. A thousand blockchains can bloom—for intangible items such as coupons and vouchers, to physical assets like cars and homes; private blockchain networks to track contracts & wills, semi-public blockchains to store & verify credentials, HR records, etc. Public blockchains for easy access to certified practitioners, land registry titles, etc., and other blockchain

networks for mobile phone SIM cards, etc. The world is awash with blockchain opportunities, and the broader applications are yet to come!

5. **Cost reduction and process improvement**: The distributed ledger and consensus mechanism provided by blockchain eliminate the need for second and third parties to validate a transaction, reducing the time and costs to settle a transaction, conduct a vote, establish a contract, etc. For several decades, business process management systems have served as a framework to simplify business processes within and across organizations and provide better transparency in a business process such as claims handling, insurance underwriting, and order to cash processes. When the data required for a business process lives in organizational silos, the conventional approach is move data between silos to support the business process. This complicated and expensive approach puts stress on integration systems and the various parties to ensure each follows the rules of engagement. For example, consider the following illustration which shows six organizations collaborating with each other during the life-cycle of a vehicle. The parties are organizations such as a manufacturer, dealer, and leasing company. Each organization maintains its information systems with a subset of data in their private databases and want to keep changes to the state of the vehicle up to date throughout the life-cycle of the vehicle.

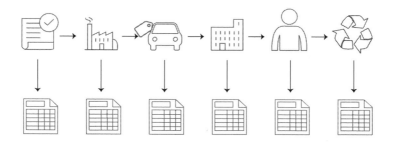

Figure 3.1: *Example automotive supply chain*

The blockchain technology can enforce the control of the transaction execution via smart contracts deployed on the blockchain.

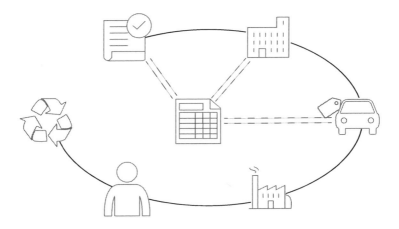

Figure 3.2: *Automotive supply chain with distributed ledger on blockchain*

A shared distributed ledger provides the interface to a single version of the truth. Participants interact with one another via message-based interfaces that follow the individual contracts between pairs of participants and rules of operation of the network. Automated transactions offer the highest potential for new services and disruption. Assurance that the asset transfer will happen only after transaction validation, reduces the need for legal, accounting and insurance services. According to a report from McKinsey, 'blockchains have the potential to dramatically reshape the capital markets industry, with significant impact on business models, reductions in risk and savings of cost and capital.'

3.5   Challenges in Enterprise Adoption

There are many technical and business challenges that continue to be a barrier to mass adoption of blockchain. These include a variety of different vendor technical initiatives, a lack of proven and diverse use cases with sound business proposition, uncertainty over governmental regulation, and a lack of skills / developer tools.

- **Technical Platform issues**: Perhaps the biggest hurdle in mass adoption of blockchain is lack a robust enterprise platform which provides the throughput required to augment existing business processes. Other technical challenges remain such as latency to validate a transaction. The confirmation latency in Bitcoin network takes about 10 minutes on average (though in reality that happens in only ~63% of the time, while ~12% of the time it will take longer than 10 minutes, and in 0.25% it can take over an hour). The transaction latency in Ethereum public is ~17 seconds. This pales when compared to enterprise systems which have requirements for processing of hundreds or even thousands of transactions per second. Other technical challenges around the size of the ledger, bandwidth required to update the ledger, scalability and storage requirements.

- **Security & privacy concerns**: If the distributed ledger records the transactions and stores confidential contractual information, it increases the attack surface for hackers to gain access. There are solutions that offer strong encryption, but integration of blockchains with existing systems requires a comprehensive security strategy for the entire business application.

- **Lack of skills**: Finding developers with the blockchain expertise is rare. Blockchain developer tools are nascent. These factors increase security risks and make the cost of developing with blockchain platforms higher than existing technology stacks.

- **Regulation**: Blockchain has potential to disrupt and radically transform commerce and governmental institutions. A decentralized approach to identity and transaction management reduces the control of governments and corporations. You can bet Government will want to regulate its adoption, which could impact the progress of blockchain solutions. Bureaucracy, lawyers, compliance, front office, back office, middle office may slow down meaningful reform implementation, or even getting a budget to expand a technology program.

- **Culture**: Changing from legacy systems is always hard. Blockchain will change business processes, models, and perhaps entire industries.

Banks today make huge profits on financial transactions. If transfers suddenly became instantaneous and worry-free, bank risk losing a lot of revenue. Cultural adoption is crucial as blockchain requires a shift to a decentralized network which needs the buy-in of its users and operators.

- **Lack of maturity of smart contracts**: The siphoning of funds from the DAO is perhaps the most public exploit of a poorly written smart contract. A recent study found 34,200 smart contracts were vulnerable to either stealing of Ether, and could even freeze or delete assets in contracts that the attackers did not own. Implementing smart contracts require a significant amount of integration work and developers need to contemplate the boundary conditions for testing the smart contracts.

3.6   Key Blockchain Technologies & Consortiums

Industry groups formed many consortiums in 2017, with most of them geared towards the financial industry. Commercial use of blockchain will promote blockchain technologies that are general purpose or industry focused. This section summarizes some of the key associations and blockchain consortiums available in the marketplace today.

Ethereum

Ethereum is a public, open source blockchain-based distributed computing platform launched in 2015, featuring smart contract functionality. It provides a decentralized virtual machine, the Ethereum Virtual Machine (EVM) that can execute peer-to-peer contracts using a cryptocurrency called ether. It has been under active development since 2014 by 30 core developers, led at a high level by Vitalik Buterin, a 20-year-old Canadian computer science prodigy with links to Peter Thiel. Buterin's aim was to create a platform for developing decentralized applications. Ethereum exists as a public, permissionless or trustless network, similar to Bitcoin. It has 32,000 nodes mining on its Mainnet at the time of writing, ~125,000 smart contracts deployed, which translates to

~125,000 solutions of various sizes (although one project can have many smart contracts) running on the Mainnet.

Ethereum intends to create an alternative protocol for building decentralized applications, via a blockchain with a built-in Turing-complete programming language, allowing anyone to write smart contracts and decentralized applications where they can create their own arbitrary rules for ownership, transaction formats, and state transition functions.

Ethereum uses the Ethereum Virtual Machine (EVM) and the Solidity programming language to implement and execute peer-to-peer and multi-party agreements among other applications. It has no centralized authority, no government body or corporation behind it, and runs wherever there is the Internet.

In Ethereum, the state comprises objects called as "accounts." There are two types of accounts-

- Externally owned accounts: There is no code with them, and private keys control them. An externally owned account can send messages to both types of accounts by creating and signing a transaction using its private key.
- Contract accounts: A contract account has an ether balance and associated code. Transactions or messages received from other contracts trigger the code execution, and contract accounts perform operations of an arbitary complexity. Contract accounts cannot start a new transaction on their own.

The Ethereum smart contracts live on the blockchain, and get activated by sending money to an address (known as 'Gas' fee), and can run the code, send transactions, change memory or even change the smart contract code. Similar to Bitcoin, Ethereum uses a Proof-Of-Work algorithm such that all transaction miners come to a consensus about what happened and what is happening to the transmission and storage of the Ether value tokens, and agreeing about all the processing done on the shared programs. It achieves the consensus in Ethereum every 17 seconds because in a distributed system the nodes are all across the globe with varying speed of Internet connectivity.

Ethereum comprises multiple components. It uses Whisper for messaging so that Dapps can communicate with each other (e.g., record an offer to sell a commodity at a specific price on an exchange). Swarm is a distributed storage platform and also provides content distribution services. The aim of Swarm is to provide redundant and decentralized storage (e.g., Dapp code and data). The Ethereum Virtual Machine (EVM) executes computations and also tracks the state of millions of objects called accounts. Tracking of "states" is a critical component of smart contracts because the platform needs to track ether balances in a way similar to a bank certifying a customer has funds in his/her account.

Figure 3.3 illustrates some key components of Ethereum:

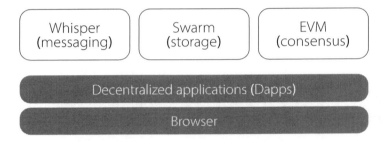

Figure 3.3: *Key components of Ethereum*

Ethereum is a global singleton as the public nodes worldwide running Ethereum form the Ethereum World Computer. The Ethereum World Computer represents a robust cryptographic foundation on which to build next-generation information and decision-making systems that are secure, non-repudiable, uncensorable and transparent.

Since its launch, Ethereum has become the world's de facto choice for developing distributed applications (called Dapps) and has facilitated the rise of Initial Coin/ Token Offerings (ICOs/ITO). Few examples of decentralized applications are a Universal Sharing Network of autonomous devices by combining blockchain with IoT (by Slock.it); platforms for prediction markets such as Augur and Gnosis; and secure identity systems such as uPort. Decentralized applications are applicable in every sector/ vertical and not just for the financial industry. They may use ether itself as its digital token or may issue tokens on top of Ethereum. However, it is important to note that transactions between Ethereum tokens are ether transactions itself from the network's perspective and need gas for execution.

Ethereum also enables building a decentralized and democratic organization called Decentralized Autonomous Organizations (DAO) that exists only on the blockchain. The governance rules of the decentralized organization are also part of the code (such as adding members and voting rules).

In May 2016, the company Slock.it created one of the first DAO. It was a complex smart contract running on Ethereum, and they funded it via a token sale in May 2016. The DAO was an investor-directed venture capital fund and provided investors with the ability to vote on future proposals.

An attacker exploited a security loophole in the DAO in June 2016 resulting in the draining of 3.6 million Ether (out of 11.5 million Ether committed to the DAO). The bug was not in the Ethereum blockchain network but in the distributed app built on top. The developers in a public blockchain network fix such issues by upgrading the client software running on the nodes to implement a change to the code. However, in certain circumstances not all nodes will upgrade the version of the blockchain code, which splits the blockchain into two (and hence the term 'fork'). To fix this issue, the Ethereum developers had a choice between two types of forks:

- **Soft Fork**: A soft fork is backward compatible and required nodes with at least 51% of the 'hashing power' to upgrade so they will take control of the new blockchain formed by the new code, forcing non-upgrading nodes to upgrade or else waste the hashing power. However, the developers found a bug in the soft fork implementation few hours before rollout of the intended fix, and so they canceled it.

- **Hard Fork**: A hard fork is backward incompatible and is a change to the protocol that splits off one part of the blockchain. In the DAO fix, they implemented a hard fork. While this forking was a pragmatic decision so they could refund the ether drained from the DAO, 'crypto-idealists' or the purists were critical since forking went against immutability of the blockchain and 'code being law.' The miners who continued to support the non-upgraded chain called their network as Ethereum Classic.

In March 2017, 30 founding members formed the Ethereum Enterprise Alliance. The guiding principles of EEA are:

1. Development of open source standards

2. Working with builders and doers towards a general purpose system

3. Maintain compatibility with public Ethereum network

4. Not reinventing the wheel on data standards

As of December 2017, EEA has almost 200 members representing almost every sector and industry including public services. The EEA is helping to evolve Ethereum into an enterprise-grade technology, providing research and development in a range of areas, including privacy, confidentiality, scalability, and security. The EEA is also investigating hybrid architectures that span both permissioned and public Ethereum networks and industry-specific application layer working groups. Within EEA there are working groups representing different verticals. Only EEA members can join one of the 14 pre-defined working groups.

Hyperledger

Hyperledger is an open-source collaborative effort created to advance cross-industry blockchain technologies. It is a global collaboration, hosted by The Linux Foundation, including leaders in finance, banking, Internet of Things, supply chain, manufacturing, and technology.

Goals

The Hyperledger project has advanced cross-industry blockchain technologies with the following objectives:

- Create enterprise-grade, open source, distributed ledger frameworks & code bases to support business transactions

- Provide a neutral, open, & community-driven infrastructures backed by technical and business governance

- Build technical communities to develop blockchain and shared ledger POCs, use cases, field trials and deployments

- Educate the public about the market opportunity for the blockchain technology

- Promote our community of communities taking a toolkit approach with many platforms and frameworks

Hyperledger has a modular umbrella approach. At the top level, The Linux Foundation and Hyperledger provide the infrastructure for open development to occur and includes technical, legal, marketing, and organizational aspects.

Under Hyperledger's umbrella are many projects that take different approaches to creating business blockchain tools and frameworks — Fabric, Iroha, Sawtooth, Burrow, and Indy.

- **Sawtooth** - Hyperledger Sawtooth is a modular platform for building, deploying, and running distributed ledgers. Hyperledger Sawtooth includes a novel consensus algorithm, Proof of Elapsed Time (PoET), which targets large, distributed transaction validator populations with minimal resource consumption.

- **Iroha** - Hyperledger Iroha is a business blockchain framework designed to be simple and easy to incorporate into infrastructural projects requiring distributed ledger technology.

- **Fabric** - Intended as a foundation for developing applications or solutions with a modular architecture, Hyperledger Fabric allows components, such as consensus and membership services, to be plug-and-play. Started with IBM, Fabric has received the lion's share of developer involvement although this has changed recently with the investments in

Sawtooth. Fabric has a modular architecture and application developers create smart contracts (called "chaincode"), which are Go scripts running inside a Docker container. They released version 1.0 of Fabric using the PBFT consensus algorithm in June 2017. Besides IBM, other contributors include Huawei, DTCC, London Stock Exchange, DAH, and a bunch of smaller startups.

- **Burrow** - Hyperledger Burrow is a permissionable smart contract machine. The first of its kind when released in December 2014, Burrow provides a modular blockchain client with a permissioned smart contract interpreter built in part to the specification of the Ethereum Virtual Machine (EVM).

- **Indy** - Hyperledger Indy is a distributed ledger, purpose-built for decentralized identity. It provides tools, libraries, and reusable components for creating and using independent digital identities rooted on blockchains or other distributed ledgers for interoperability.

Hyperledger Fabric

Hyperledger Fabric is a blockchain framework implementation and one of the Hyperledger projects hosted by The Linux Foundation. Intended as a foundation for developing applications or solutions with a modular architecture, Hyperledger Fabric allows components, such as consensus and membership services, to be plug-and-play. Hyperledger Fabric leverages container technology to host smart contracts called "chaincode" that comprise the application logic of the system.

Here are high-level goals of Hyperledger Fabric project:

- **Private and Permissioned**. Members of a Hyperledger Fabric network enroll through a Membership Services Provider (MSP).

- **Extensible & Pluggable** architecture Hyperledger Fabric offers several pluggable options. It can store ledger data in multiple formats, offers switching of consensus mechanisms, and it supports different MSPs.

- **Shared Ledger**. Hyperledger Fabric has a ledger subsystem comprising two components: the world state and the transaction log. Each participant has a copy of the ledger to every Hyperledger Fabric network they belong to. The world state component describes the state of the ledger at a point in time. It's the database of the ledger. The transaction log component records all transactions which have resulted in the current value of the world state. It's the update history for the world state. The ledger comprises the world state database and the transaction log history.

- **The smart contracts** in Hyperledger Fabric are called chaincode and an application external to the blockchain invokes them when that application needs to interact with the ledger. In most cases chaincode only interacts with the database component of the ledger, the world state (querying it, for example), and not the transaction log.

- **Privacy of participants in the network**: There are scenarios where some participants in the network will want to transact with others but do not want rest of the network to have details about the transactions. Fabric provides this capability via Channels.

- **Consensus**: Hyperledger Fabric writes transactions to the ledger in the order in which they occur, even though they might be between different participants within the network. The network establishes the transaction order and has a method for rejecting erroneous and malicious transactions.

Corda

Formed in 2014, Corda is a distributed ledger platform developed by R3, geared towards the financial world. Although blockchain inspires it, Corda is a distributed ledger and not a blockchain.

Corda's vision is a 'global logical ledger' with which all actors interact and one that allows any parties to record and manage transactions amongst themselves in a secure, consistent, reliable, private and authoritative manner. It differs from a blockchain in that an end-state of Corda is one where everybody sees the same data that pertains to them, but the physical implementation and storage of the ledger is different as compared to blockchain.

The global ledger in Corda is a reliable single source, but the transactions and ledger entries are not visible globally. Where transactions only involve a small subgroup of parties, Corda strives to keep the relevant data within that subgroup.

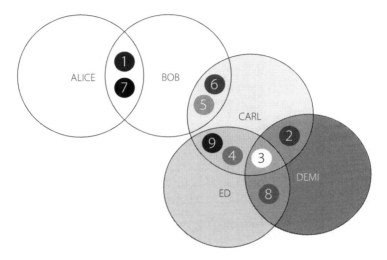

Figure 3.4: *Corda global logical ledger*

In the figure 3.4 above, the five circles represent five different peers in Corda. Carl, Demi, and Ed know of shared fact 3, Alice and Bob are not. Alice and Bob may not have facts they don't know about in their physical copies of the ledger.

To summarize Corda:

- There is no "central ledger."

- Each network peer maintains a separate vault of facts (similar to rows in a database table)

- All peers of a shared fact store identical copies.

- Not all on-ledger facts are shared with other peers.

- The ledger is immutable. It is easy to analyze a static snapshot of the data and reason about the contents.

- Transaction ordering: It is impossible to mis-order transactions due to reliance on hash functions to identify previous states.

- Consensus: it establishes transaction validity and uniqueness before committing an update to produce a new state.

Key Concepts

1. The fundamental object in Corda is a *state object* which is a digital document which records the existence, content and current state of an agreement between two or more parties. It defines the ledger as a set of immutable state objects, and Corda's aim is to ensure that all parties to the agreement remain in consensus 'as to this state as it evolves'. Corda's focus on states of agreement is in contrast to systems where data over which participants must reach consensus represents the state of an entire ledger or the state of an entire virtual machine.

2. Corda applies updates to the ledger using transactions, which consume existing state objects and produce new objects. It commits a transaction proposal only if it:

3. Doesn't contain double-spends

4. Is contractually valid

5. Is signed by the required parties

6. Consensus is the mechanism via which transactions achieve both validity and uniqueness, to ensure contractual validity and prevent double spending. Parties can agree on transaction validity by independently running the same contract code and validation logic, but consensus over transaction uniqueness requires a pre-determined, independent observer.

7. Flows are lightweight processes used to automate the process of agreeing ledger updates.

CHAPTER 4

EXAMPLE ENTERPRISE APPLICATIONS

In this chapter, I discuss enterprise applications based on blockchain from around the world. I have selected applications from across various industries—financial institutions, retail, transportation, and logistics, etc., to provide a flavor of the innovative applications possible with blockchain.

4.1 Food Traceability

The tracking of food supply chain to establish the veracity of the produce, it's handling and processing, and to establish provenance is critical to finding and helping address the sources of contamination in the food supply chain worldwide.

When applied to the food supply chain, blockchain can store digital product information (such as farm origination details, batch numbers, factory and processing data, expiration dates, storage temperatures and shipping details) along every step of the process.

All members of the business network agree upon the information captured in each transaction; once there is a consensus, it becomes a permanent record that no one can alter. Each piece of information provides critical data that might reveal food safety issues with the product. The record created by the blockchain can also help retailers better manage the shelf-life of products in individual stores and further strengthen safeguards related to food authenticity.

Contaminants that make people sick are a culprit of consumer woes and can be a costly issue for grocers to tackle. "It's been reported that a 1% reduction in food-borne disease in the U.S. would amount to about a $700 billion saving to the U.S. economy," according to Frank Yiannas, VP of food safety, Walmart. "But it's more than just cost; it's people. The CDC [Centers for Disease Control] estimates that about 48 million Americans will experience foodborne illness in the U.S., and the global numbers are even larger."

IBM and Walmart worked together to perform the test on Chinese pork, and US mangoes, which proved that they could now trace food origins, a process which once took weeks in 2.2 seconds. They tracked products with blockchain technology through scans as they traveled from farms to Walmart shelves, recording various pertinent product details on an immutable ledger.

In this application, all participants on the food supply chain—from the farmer or breeder to manufacturer, distribution centers, retail stores, consumers and auditors, all have an association with the data stored on the blockchain.

- Breeders or Farmers can provide information securely on the raw materials or feed used in the farms, type of fertilizer used, audit logs from visits from food safety inspectors, etc.

- Manufacturers provide information about the machinery used, and the processing performed at the farm including adherence to food safety standards such as NSF and HAACP. They also create product packages with electronic bar code based information labels for use by regulators and consumers.

- Distributors may aggregate products into bundles, or disaggregate packages for distribution into retail stores.

- Retail stores have full visibility into the product packages across transport lines.

- Consumers have visibility at the checkout till, or via mobile app, and can view the compliance data for any product including judging the veracity of meats, organic produce, etc.

- Auditors and food safety inspectors have end-to-end visibility of each product path across the supply chain, and check compliance of machinery to food safety standards, certify the food supply chain and generate audit records.

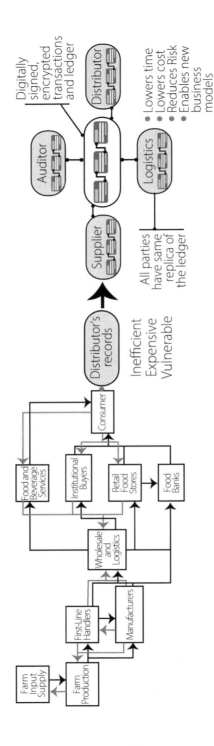

Figure 4.1: *Food traceability with blockchain: Technology & Implications*

Benefits

"The benefits are many," Yiannis said. "When people talk about the food safety benefits, for example, when there's a food scandal - often what will happen is health officials will say we've seen illnesses documented in the country, and we think consumers shouldn't eat, for example, spinach."

"What happens is everybody's guilty until proven innocent, all of this product comes off of the shelf, it incriminates everybody," he said. "When the dust settles you find out it was one supplier, maybe one production line - so if you could identify this, you could target and remove the product and protect people from getting ill."

Other benefits include:

- Supplier / Vendor Information and Certifications and associated Product certifications will be on the Blockchain

    - e.g., Supplier Certification during registration—(Supplier Identity)

    - e.g., Product Certification during product creation and transfer to transport

- Product date/batch code, shelf-life/expiration date, and factory information can be stored on the QR-Code and on the blockchain. Testing information can also be stored on the blockchain.

- 3rd parties can also use the app to store the inspection reports on the blockchain; they can retrieve a product and associated report using smart contracts and checked for validity

- Products will be aggregated and disaggregated on the blockchain, with barcode scan events

- Package scans by trucking companies at various points can register the current location/state of goods on the Blockchain

- They can impose different regulations at different locations by writing regulations as Smart Contracts

Walmart expects consumers could interact with labels on their food, perhaps using a smartphone app, to bring up the journey of the product and any other information they want to see. This would require the active participation of many other big players in the food industry to work. The food supply chain is a complex food system, there is a lot of actors and players in it, and a blockchain solution for food transparency needs to be collaborative, and the project wants as many people in food production to be involved and engaged in it.

4.2   Diamond tracking and fraud prevention

Authenticity and transparency is everything in the world of luxury goods. Risk emerges when provenance is broken, and risk fuels the three biggest black markets: theft, fraud, and cybercrime. Risk allows for the movement and trafficking of counterfeit goods across international borders and the proliferation of commodities like blood diamonds that help to fund terrorism around the world.

According to the Association of British Insurers, 65% of fraudulent claims go undetected costing the industry over £45 billion per year. Knowing a precious stone's origin can stop fencing and insurance frauds and winnow out synthetic diamonds or those sourced in war zones. But forged paper certificates make provenance hard to verify. The diamond trade is marred by fraud and worse, as nefarious actors often trade rough diamonds out of conflict zones to fund violent insurgencies in places like Sierra Leone, Liberia, and Angola.

In 2000, the UN adopted the Kimberley Process: a rough diamond certification system widely adopted to stamp out the trade of so-called 'blood diamonds', by demanding proper documentation for any stones shipped out of 80 selected regions. Its goal is to promote the trading of diamonds from legitimate sources and to ensure that consumers can be confident in the origin of their diamond purchases.

Tracking a diamond from the mine to the retail store is a tricky process and is far from perfect. There are many parties involved in the business network—workers, the mining company, sorting, distribution & trading agencies, cutting & polishing companies, distributors, and retailers. The diamonds are sent for certification after mining and cutting. Certificate houses inspect the diamonds, while laboratories grade them using the 4C's - cut, carat, clarity, and color. Certification houses then serialize the stones and issue physical certificates with all the attributes of the diamond, including the girdle dimensions and hand-drawn line pictures. These certificates follow the diamonds into retail chains and increase the price of the stones considerably. While the Kimberly Process is a paper-based and prone to tampering by the parties in the supply chain,

Everledger aims to create a global digital registry for diamonds, powered by the blockchain. Everledger creates a digital thumbprint for each diamond, using the four c's besides over 40+ metadata points, linking this information to the laser inscription on the bottom of the stone. Combined with high definition photography, they write all of this data onto the blockchain creating a permanent, digital thumbprint of an item.

Figure 4.2: *Diamond supply chain*

"Blockchain is immutable; it cannot be changed, so records are permanently stored," says Kemp. "Information on the blockchain is cryptographically proven by a federated consensus, instead of being written by just one person."
With this information, Everledger knows who owns which diamond and where it is. It can even trace the movement of diamonds on platforms such as eBay and Amazon as they are bought and sold. Everledger works with insurance companies when diamonds are reported stolen, and alongside Interpol and Europol where diamonds are crossing borders and entering black markets. The incentive for insurance companies to get involved is to reduce claims fraud and also recoup costs associated with paying out claims.

CREATING A DIGITAL THUMBPRINT

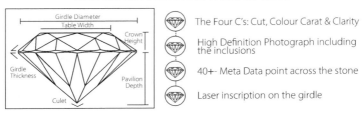

Figure 4.3: *Creating a digital thumbprint*

4.3   Dispute Resolution for Commercial Financing

IBM Global Financing (IGF) is the world's largest technology financier with over 125,000 clients in 60 countries. IGF provides channel financing for a worldwide network of over 4,000 suppliers and partners where partners get a credit line to purchase from the suppliers. In 2014 IGF financed $44 billion in over 2.9 million transactions. About 25,000 disputes arise per year over issues such as the wrong number of computer parts in an order or deliveries that go awry. Up to $100 million in capital is tied up in disputes, with average disputed invoice amount of $31,000.

The information about a transaction is split among many parties, so no one has a clear view of the entire transaction. It it takes an average of 44 days to resolve such issues. Employees use six to seven software applications to verify steps taken in the arrangement and having to call banks, financial institutions, and associated partners.

Without blockchain, participants in the transaction:

- Lack end-to-end visibility, from invoice to cash

- Use incompatible systems

- Have no end-to-end view of the progress of goods and payment

- Have to launch a dispute to resolve issues

- Waste time, tie up money and strain relationships

The IGF blockchain solution brings all the partners, suppliers and IGF to use the same distributed ledger so all participants have access to the most up-to-date version of the truth.

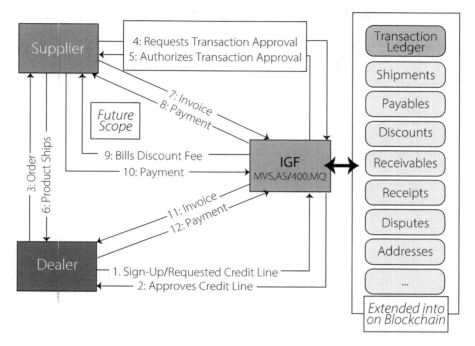

Figure 4.4: *IBM Global Financing on Blockchain*

1. When a partner places an order, they add the PO information on the blockchain

2. The supplier may approve or reject The transaction

3. IGF verifies approval on blockchain and provides credit

4. The supplier sends the shipment. All participants have insight into the status.

5. Supplier submits the invoice to IGF

6. IGF initiates a remittance to the supplier

7. All participants can verify proof of delivery by the supplier

8. Upon proof of delivery, IGF notifies partner of payment due.

9. Partner issues payment to IGF

With blockchain, participants in the transaction:

- Share a single platform with permissioned and secure access

- Receive a full view of the process

- Easily track from purchase order to product delivery

- Can drill down to see all steps in the process

- Can see exact moment when a delay or error occurs

- Remedy problems without filing a dispute

- Achieve on-boarding and quick installation without disruption

Using blockchain improves many key operational parameters such as capital settlement time, the number of disputes, and time to resolve the dispute. The resulting capital efficiency and a reduction in working capital are the key benefits of the blockchain solution.

4.4 Global Trade Digitization

Ninety percent of goods in global trade is carried by the ocean shipping industry each year. Maersk found in 2014 that just a single shipment of refrigerated goods from East Africa to Europe can go through nearly 30 people and organizations, including over 200 different interactions and communications among them. Inefficiencies plague global supply chains by:

- Ineffective information sharing across organizational boundaries.

- Manual, paper-based processes.

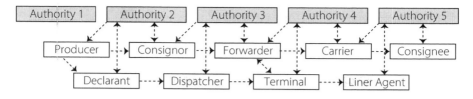

Figure 4.5: *Shipping industry process today*

The shipping industry process today is a complex system where actors are communicating back and forth and data is stored locally at each actor's site

The participants in the global supply chain face several key challenges:

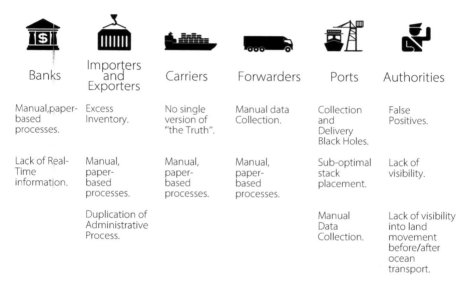

Banks	Importers and Exporters	Carriers	Forwarders	Ports	Authorities
Manual,paper-based processes.	Excess Inventory.	No single version of "the Truth".	Manual data Collection.	Collection and Delivery Black Holes.	False Positives.
Lack of Real-Time information.	Manual, paper-based processes.	Manual, paper-based processes.	Manual, paper-based processes.	Sub-optimal stack placement.	Lack of visibility.
	Duplication of Administrative Process.			Manual Data Collection.	Lack of visibility into land movement before/after ocean transport.

Figure 4.6: *Global supply chain challenges*

IBM and Maersk together are building a global solution for sharing trade data among ecosystem partners designed to transform the international supply chain. The solution will not only digitize the entire supply chain process but enhance transparency and the highly secure sharing of information to provide a more integrated flow of data among trading partners, financial institutions, governments and logistics companies.

The Global Trade Digitization solution, built using blockchain, is an immutable, secure and trusted shared network. They use it for tracking exchanges of critical information and documentation such as records of inspection, bills of lading, customs documents and final receipt of goods. Throughout the transaction, each participant has access to end-to-end visibility across the supply chain, based on their level of permission. The new solution will manage and track over 10 million shipping containers, providing an unprecedented level of transparency and trust that will help reduce or eliminate fraud and errors, reduce the time products spend in the transit and shipping process, improve inventory management, and reduce waste and cost.

Figure 4.7: *IBM and Maersk Global Trade Digitization Platform*

Some participants of the solution include:

- Customs Administration of the Netherlands who had been looking to expedite the customs and export processes for years. This is a way for the government to play a leading role in empowering smaller players to enter the global trading economy.

- A Maersk Line container vessel transports goods from Schneider Electric from the Port of Rotterdam to the Port of Newark in a live shipment using the solution.

- S. Customs and Border Protection took part on the receiving end of the live shipment.

- Damco, Maersk's freight forwarding company, supported origin management activities of the shipment while using the solution.

- The solution was developed in close cooperation with the European Commission services (Directorate-General Migration and Home Affairs and the Directorate-General for Taxation and Customs Union), under the EU FP7 CORE demonstrator project.

Potential benefits for supply chain actors because of adoption of blockchain:

 Authorities

- Improved efficiency and reduced admin cost (reduced communication and compliance time)

- Trade boost (tax revenue, political perception)

 Forwarders

- Gain market share by improved service offering to customers- e.g., supply chain visibility

- Reduced costs of existing services to customers

 Shipping lines

- Access to direct customers, increased share of waller, improved service offering

- Cost savings from reduced waiting time, admin costs, compliance costs

 Terminals

- Increased marker share in competitive ports

- Reduced administrative costs

- Increased available capacity from improved efficiency and fewer inspections

 Importers/Exporters

- Ability to differentiate by responding faster to shifts in market supply/demand

- Improved tracking of consignments

- Lower variance of transportation time, reducing warehousing cost

 Inland transportation

- Increased marker share through improved service

- Reduced waiting time due to admin delay, increasing available capacity

Figure 4.8: *Benefits of adopting block for global shipping industry*

4.5   Blockchain Solution for Derivatives Processing

The Depository Trust and Clearing Corporation (DTCC) is the central book-keeper for Wall Street's securities trades. DTCC provides a Trade Information Warehouse (TIW) service which automates the record keeping, life-cycle events, and payment management for more than $11 trillion of cleared and bilateral credit derivatives (98% of all Credit Derivatives traded worldwide). Over 2,500 buy-side firms such as mutual funds and pension funds in over 70 countries use the TIW service.

In the current process of derivates processing, TIW is a central warehouse where the metadata about the trades lives–things such as the type of instrument (equity, bond, or warrant), issue details (short name, long name, size, denomination, etc.) exchange rates, currency information, and other information. TIW keeps a copy of the record, and each of the participants also trades within their ledgers, and they reconcile between DTCC's records and their records. This makes it a complex process where multiple parties have to agree to the same information and require a complex reconciliation process to arrive at a mutual consensus in processing the transactions.

DTCC decided in 2017 to re-platform the TIW solution, in partnership with IBM, Axoni, and R3 through a distributed ledger technology framework to drive improvements in the derivates post-trade life cycle events. This will enable DTCC and its clients to further automate and reduce the cost of derivatives processing across the industry by removing disjointed, redundant processing capabilities and associated reconciliation costs. They will deploy the solution in several stages, with an "end-state vision" to establish a permissioned distributed ledger network (i.e., private) for derivatives - governed by industry-owned DTCC with peer nodes at taking part firms. They have developed it with input from several big banks including Barclays, Citi, Credit Suisse, Deutsche Bank, J.P. Morgan and UBS and key market infrastructure providers, IHS Markit and Intercontinental Exchange.

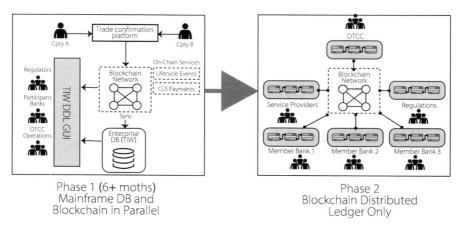

Phase 1 (6+ moths)
Mainframe DB and
Blockchain in Parallel

Phase 2
Blockchain Distributed
Ledger Only

Figure 4.9: *Vision for processing of credit derivates on blockchain.* SOURCE: PHASE 1 AND 2 DIAGRAMS FROM IBM

The phased solution approach depicted in the picture above shows a pragmatic approach to run the distributed ledger version of the service and database in parallel with the existing version of the TIW service, processing and storing trades on both platforms. Once the project has achieved confidence in robustness and scale, DTCC will decommission the legacy TIW platform and progress to phase 2, which includes participant adoption of nodes on the distributed ledger network.

DTCC confirmed that although the ledger is distributed, DTCC will continue to play the role of central authority, which has several benefits. They can ensure well-defined processes for code deployment, and access controls mechanisms and permissioning. This central governance is vital for the confidence of market participants and the regulatory community.

4.6 Digital ID and Authentication

The first e-commerce website appeared over 20 years ago, yet we still use the same username, password and security question combinations to log in online. Human resources departments are filled with paper files of photocopied passports and Social Security cards. And, just like more than half a century ago, someone going to a bar still has to show a stranger a driver's license full of identifiable information (name, address, date of birth) to prove they are old enough to drink.

The methods for managing identities in this digital age is antiquated. It's inefficient, as consumers and businesses re-enter the same information to access many services. At worst, it's dangerous, as the many high-profile data breaches of the past several years show.

Banks see themselves are stewards of identity – they would serve as authenticators. A single, federated identity would provide several benefits:

- It would be much easier for the banks to know who they are dealing with if they could get quick access to a token or digital certificate that established a person's identity.

- Regulatory compliance would be easier and cheaper (both regarding money spent and internal resources dedicated to this task) to adhere to processes such as KYC

- Improved security since personal information would not be strewn across multiple systems in multiple banks eliminating the number of systems that require encryption, PII compliance, etc.

There are many benefits for consumers/end user as well:

- Control the aspects of their ID that would be shared between banks or divisions of a bank. For example, the app could vouch that a customer is old enough to drink in a pub, so they don't have to show a driver's license with an exact birthdate, or confirm their last three addresses to a landlord, saving both parties time spent looking up old lease documents or checking references.

- Individuals need not provide all personal information every time they consume a new bank service since they KYC information they have provided to avail a service from a bank can be reused repeatedly.

- Reduced risk of loss of personal data due to potential hacks or breaches at different providers (financial institutions or other e-commerce websites).

Most people re-use the same username/password combination across websites so once a breach happens, the proportional risk of loss of data on other websites increases.

SecureKey Technologies partnered with IBM to enable a new digital identity and attribute sharing network based on blockchain. The network makes it easier for consumers to verify they are who they say they are, in a privacy-enhanced, security-rich and efficient way. Consumers can use the network to verify their identity for services such as a new bank accounts, driver's licenses or utilities.

Once it goes in 2017 Canadian consumers will opt-in to the new blockchain-based service using a mobile app. Consumers – or network members – will control what identifying the information they share from trusted credentials to the organizations of their choice, so that those organizations can validate the consumer's identity and arrange new services. For example, if a consumer has proven their identity with their bank and a credit agency, they can grant permission to share their data with a utility to create a new account. Since the bank and the credit agency have already gone through extensive verification of the consumer's identity, the utility can rely on the fact that the information is verified, and they can approve the consumer for new services.

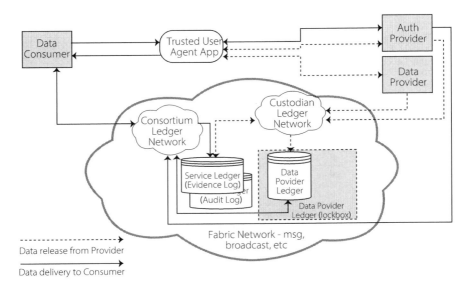

Figure 4.10: *The Concierge Identity System*

Canada's leading banks, including BMO, CIBC, Desjardins, RBC, Scotiabank, and TD joined the digital identity ecosystem in October 2016, investing $27M in SecureKey. The Digital ID and Authentication Council of Canada (DIACC) and the Command Control and Interoperability Center for Advanced Data Analytics (CCICADA), a research center of excellence funded by the U.S. Department of Homeland Security Science & Technology Directorate, have also funded bring the new approach to digital identity to market. SecureKey's leadership in Identity is clear by its association with industry leaders and regulators such as DIACC, Privacy By Design, NIST, FIDO, OIX, Kantara and the Linux Foundation.

CHAPTER 5

ARCHITECTURAL CONSIDERATIONS OF BLOCKCHAIN

In this chapter I will talk about the areas of interest to enterprises impacted by blockchain, or considerations when designing blockchain solutions. But first, we should get a first grasp of a typical blockchain application and the mechanisms used to interact with it.

5.1 Anatomy of a blockchain application

Table 5.1 describes the various participants and their roles in a blockchain application:

Blockchain Architect	The Blockchain Architect is responsible for the overall architecture of the solution.
Blockchain User	The Blockchain User is someone who is consuming the solution, and in most cases, not aware that blockchain technology is in use. For example, consider a food safety application in the retail supply chain that uses blockchain for tracking produce from farm to the store. The end-user may be provided a mobile application which they use to scan the produce in the grocery aisle of a retail store and obtain information about the item without realizing the technology used behind the scenes.

Blockchain Regulator	The Blockchain Regulator operates as an overall authority within the network and may have broad access to contents of the ledger in the network. The Blockchain Regulator is a role who's eventual permissions are agreed upon by the network participants. Some regulators may only want read permissions on all the records on the ledger. Other regulators may require write access to the ledger or perhaps admin access to manage part of the business, e.g., to allocate quotas or codes for different banks or even enroll participants or deactivate peers. The role and associated permissions of the Blockchain Regulator are dependent on the network rules, and they do not have a fixed/standard definition or set of permissions that fits all.
Blockchain Developer	Blockchain Developers are responsible for building the application and writing of the smart contracts.
Blockchain Operator	Blockchain Operators manage and monitor the blockchain network. Each business participant is a blockchain operator represented by one or more nodes on the network.
Membership Services	Membership Service is a component that aims to offer an abstraction of a membership operation architecture. In Hyperledger Fabric, Membership Services Provider component provides both identity validation and authentication. Membership Services component is responsible for mapping digital credentials to identities that have a meaning in the context of the blockchain network. Without it, the CA issuing certificates that does not have any significance in a blockchain network.
Traditional Processing Platform	One or more existing computer systems used by the blockchain for integration purposes or to augment the processing of business rules associated with the network.
Traditional Data Sources	One or more existing data repositories which may provide data to influence the outcome of smart contracts.

Table 5.1: *Participants and roles in blockchain application*

Figure 5.1 provides a high-level overview of the anatomy of a typical blockchain application.

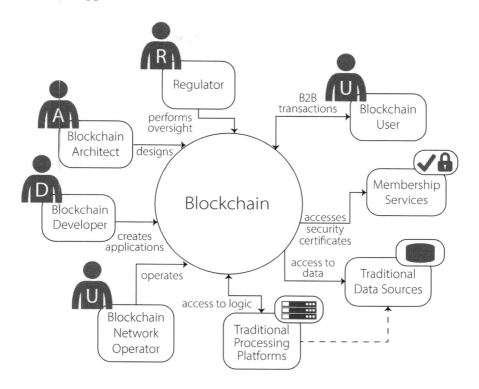

Figure 5.1: *Anatomy of a blockchain application*

5.2   Blockchain application and the Ledger

The ledger in blockchain often has two data structures:

1. Blockchain itself – a linked list of blocks such that each block describes a set of transactions and is immutable.

2. The World State – a key-value data store which stores the combined output of all transactions thus representing the current state of the blockchain. The World State is not immutable and thus allows for 'delete' operations on the blockchain. The World State datastore provides a

means to determine the ownership of all assets and participants rather than traversing the entire blockchain.

Figure 5.2 provides an example of interaction with the ledger.

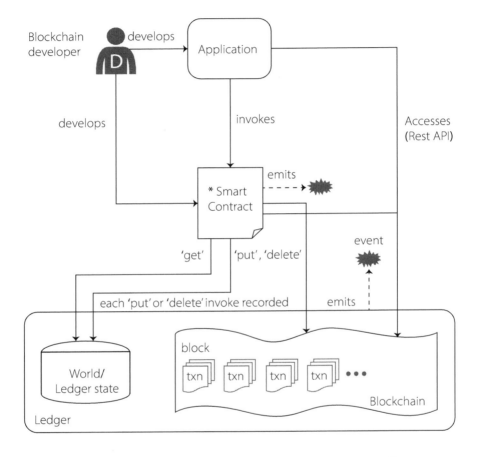

Figure 5.2: *Example blockchain application interaction flow*

- One or more developers create an application and smart contract

- The application invokes calls within the smart contract

- The business logic within the smart contract processes those calls

- A 'put' or 'delete' command goes through consensus protocol selected and added to the blockchain.

- A 'get' command can only read from the world state but is not stored on the blockchain.

- A smart contract must use the APIs in the same way an application would read from the blockchain.

- A 'delete' operation can only delete from the World state, not the blockchain. The ledger's current state data represents the latest values for all keys ever included in the chain transaction log.

The application focuses on the blockchain user's business needs and experience. It calls the smart contracts for interactions with the ledger state. The application can access ledger transactions directly, if required (for example, 'read' transactions from the ledger) and can also process events if required.

A Smart Contract encapsulates business logic, written in the implementation languages supported by the blockchain fabric (for example, Ethereum supports Solidity, Hyperledger supports Golang and JavaScript). The Smart Contract developers define appropriate interfaces for interaction with the attributes of the assets stored in the ledger. For example, Smart Contracts may support interfaces such as getOwner(), or updateOwner(). The interfaces exposed by Smart Contracts access the ledger state ensuring consistent read and writes. Each invocation of a Smart Contract is a 'blockchain transaction' and is stored on the blockchain.

The Ledger state (also known as 'world state') holds the current value of smart contract data. For example, in an automotive network blockchain, the world state may have vehicleOwner=Daisy. The blockchain holds the historical sequence of all smart contract transactions. For example, it will store the state change of ownership for a vehicle:

```
updateOwner(from=John, to=Anthony); updateOwner (from=Anthony,
    to=Daisy)
```

5.3 Permissioned Blockchain Network Overview

Figure 5.3 depicts an example permissioned blockchain network, which features a distributed, decentralized peer-to-peer architecture, and a Certificate Authority managing user roles and permissions:

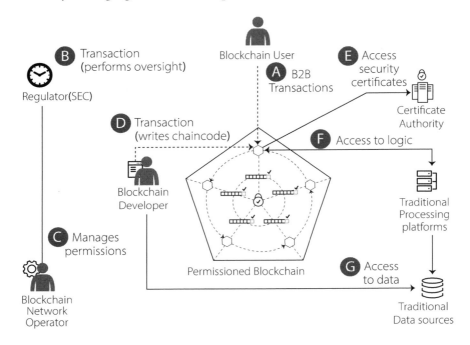

Figure 5.3: *A permissioned blockchain network*

The following descriptions correspond to the architecture and flow shown in Figure 1 (note: these do not represent a sequential process):

1. Blockchain User submits a transaction to the Blockchain network. The transaction can be a deploy, invoke or query, and is issued through a client-side application leveraging an SDK, or through a REST API.

2. Trusted business networks provide access to regulators and auditors (the SEC in a U.S. equities market, for example).

3. Blockchain Network Operator manages member permissions such as enrolling the Regulator (B) as an "auditor" and the Blockchain User (A)

80

as a "client." Permisssions coiuld restrict an auditor only to querying the ledger while it could allow a client to deploy, invoke, and query certain types of chaincode.

4. Blockchain Developer writes chaincode and client-side applications. The Blockchain Developer can deploy chaincode to the network through a REST interface. To include credentials from a traditional data source in chaincode, the developer could use an out-of-band connection to access the data (G).

5. Blockchain User connects to the network through a peer node (A). Before proceeding with any transactions, the node retrieves the user's enrollment and transaction certificates from the Certificate Authority. Users must possess these digital certificates to transact on a permissioned network.

6. A user trying to invoke chaincode has to verify their credentials on a traditional data source (G). The chaincode can use an out-of-band connection to this data through a traditional processing platform to confirm the user's authorization.

Let us now examine the impact of blockchain with typical considerations for enterprise applications.

5.4   Integration with existing systems

Organizations have existing systems known as Systems of Record (SOR) which are authoritative sources of an organization's data. Large organizations deploy this on traditional platforms or cloud computing environments and may process billions of transactions a day at millisecond speed with high volume, high throughput and high qualities of service.

A business network may use blockchain to track the lifecycle of an asset along with the interactions among the participants in a network – be it a car, financial instrument or tracking provenance of food. The goal is to share data across multiple enterprises in an auditable, immutable way.

There are four ways in which blockchain can integrate with SOR:

1. An enterprise wants to share SOR data with external parties and leave a record of that data exchange.

2. An existing system makes a call into the blockchain network invoking a smart contract.

3. An event on the blockchain generates a need to interact with a participant's SOR. That blockchain event may trigger the start of a transaction in the enterprise's SOR.

4. An external system event is triggered which may need to be recorded on the blockchain.

The following diagram summarizes the mechanisms available for integration blockchain with existing enterprise systems:

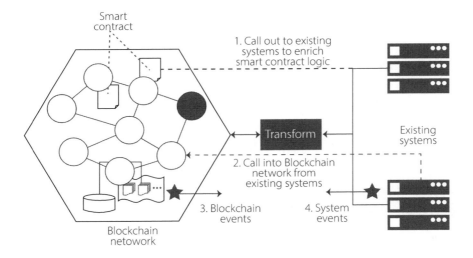

Figure 5.4: *Methods for blockchain to integrate with external systems*

A consideration that developers have to make when writing applications that will call upon external systems is the external system may not always give the same result to every blockchain node that makes the call. If the results received by the smart contract on each node taking part in a blockchain transaction are different, the nodes will not arrive at a consensus. If each smart contract calls out to an external system to receive information or uses a non-deterministic variable, it will prevent consensus being achieved. Therefore developers must take care while writing smart contracts to ensure predictability – the transaction must return the same output each time it executes.

All external data sources should return the same result for the same calls and variables must be deterministic, the smart contract code must define any non-deterministic values as part of the transaction.

There may also be a need to transform the data between blockchain and existing systems' formats. Developers may use Generic Business Objects or Application Specific Business Objects to exchange application specific data objects with smart contracts on the blockchain. A more robust approach would be to use an API Gateway integration pattern to bridge the data between the two different formats (in blockchain and existing systems).

5.5   Security

Blockchains might help improve various aspects of enterprise security such as confidentiality, transaction and identity privacy, prevention of fraudulent activities through consensus mechanisms, and detection of data tampering. They can derive several benefits from the underlying characteristics of immutability, transparency, auditability, encryption and operational resilience.

Authentication, Authorization and Access

Ensuring that only validated and allowed parties can access only appropriate data is a common concern for all organizations. It requires robust authentication, authorization, and access to control the resources available to participants in a blockchain network.

The first process of authentication provides a way of identifying a user. Permissioned blockchains will provide identity services that manage user IDs and authenticate all participants on the network. Access Control Lists (ACLs) can provide additional layers of permission through authorization of specific network operations. For example, they could permit a specific user ID to invoke a chaincode, but block it from deploying new chaincode.

Privacy and Confidentiality

While the participants may know each other's IDs, they rarely want everyone to know what they are doing. Therefore, blockchains require a measure of privacy to preserve confidentiality for certain type of operations.

For example, if Party A and Party B have a business relationship, they may engage in multiple transactions. Let's say Party A buys an asset from Party B and the two parties agree to a 6-month payment plan. After six months, there may be several transactions between the two parties which take up space on the blockchain. All that the parties may want to store on the blockchain is the outcome as a single transaction.

Blockchains such as Hyperledger and Ethereum provide a mechanism called channels, while enables competing business interests, and allow any groups that require private, confidential transactions to exist on the same permissioned network. This private two-way pathway between enables the participants to sign the transactions with their private keys to ensure they are true and authorized, but only select participants know about them. The content of the channels can be anonymous and near instant. Once a channel is closed, the underlying blockchain protocol can upload the transaction history into the ledger for the outcome to become official.

All data, including transaction, member and channel information, on a channel, are invisible and inaccessible to any network members not granted access to that channel.

Data Access

If an attacker gains access to a blockchain network and the data, this does not mean the attacker can read or retrieve the information. The network participants can apply full encryption of the data blocks and to data exchanged in transactions to guarantee its confidentiality, assuming the blockchain techno-logy follows the latest encryption standards.

Using encryption keys with PKI can provide organizations with a higher level of security. Blockchain developers have to provide a means to share the decryption keys before calling any smart contracts that need to manipulate the data stored on the blockchain. Most organizations will prefer to externalize encryption keys and integration the blockchain identity provider with an external key management solution.

Cryptographic techniques such as homomorphic encryption and zero--knowledge proofs provide another approach to privacy. These techniques perform specific computations without revealing the inputs and outputs of those computations. In a blockchain, the techniques can hide a transaction's asset quantities from all but the sender and recipient of that transaction, while still enabling all network participants to verify that the transaction is valid.

Traceability

Every transaction added to the blockchain has a signature and has a timestamp. This means that the organizations can trace every transaction back to a specific time and identify the corresponding party on the blockchain (via their ID on the blockchain network). This feature ensures non-repudiation – the ability to ensure that a party to a contract or communication cannot deny the authenticity of their signature on a document or the sending of a message they originated.

To summarize, there are various aspects of security when deploying block-chain applications:

1. Segregate the blockchain network into channels, where each channel represents a subset of participants allowed to see the data for the smart contracts they deploy that to that channel.

2. Hash or encrypt the data before calling a smart contract. If hashing is used, provide a mechanism to share the source data. If encryption is used, provide a means to share the decryption keys.

3. Use ACLs to restrict the data access to select roles in the organization by integration ACLs into the smart contract logic.

4. File system encryption on peer nodes encrypts the ledger data at rest, and TLS encrypts data-in-transit.

Figure 5.5 depicts permissioned ledger access.

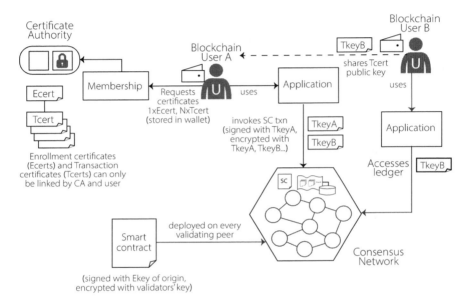

Figure 5.5: *Permissioned Ledger Access*

1. User A authenticates with the Certificate Authority which grants it membership after checking the user's credentials. The network grants user A an enrollment certificate (called 'Ecert') and multiple transaction certificates (called 'Tcert'), which user A stores in the wallet for use for signing transactions.

2. UserA and UserB agree to communicate over a private channel and userB shares her Tcert's public key, TkeyB.

3. User A signs transactions with transaction certification TkeyA, and encrypted with TkeyA and TkeyB.

4. User B accesses the ledger by providing the private key for TkeyB to authenticate itself and decrypt the transaction data.

5.6   Considerations for Blockchain Developer, Operator and Architect

The Blockchain Developer

The blockchain developer develops the application which interacts with the blockchain network, decisions on data element storage on the ledger, and writing of smart contracts for the successful operation of the blockchain network.

When designing blockchain applications, the developers must keep in mind that almost everyone is new to the blockchain, with varying degrees of skepticism and knowledge about the technology. Consumers expect the application to be reliable and wish to know the application uses blockchain even when they don't care about the technology. Good blockchain applications have three elements to their design:

1. Careful data exposure – As end-users interact with the underlying blockchain network, the expectation is that the application informs them of the API calls it makes to the network, and the UI displays information about the data sent to the network.

2. Consistency – End-users expect visual consistency across the user experience so they can trust the application, and the new technology of blockchain.

3. Communication – The blockchain application may find users beyond the identified user population (and sometimes, there is a variance of knowledge even in targeted user population). Blockchain developers must design applications that provide constant feedback to all end-user personas throughout the interaction lifecycle.

Smart contracts remain the most complex, and sensitive aspect of developing blockchain applications. Smart contract development has a lot in common with microservices development and similar design considerations apply.

1. Design for failure – Any non-trivial smart contracts will have to handle edge conditions and should fail gracefully. Blockchain developers must consider the use of design patterns such as circuit breaker pattern from the microservices world, to manage the risks associated with the smart contract.

2. Test-driven development – Test-driven development (TDD) is software development method which turns system requirements into specific test cases and the developers write the code to pass the new tests in an iterative manner. It is good practice to use TDD to develop smart contracts.

3. Externalize business logic – Smart contracts for any business network may have to make decisions that are based on business processes. In such situations, it is best to externalize business logic into an Operational Decision Management system and keep the smart contract simple. Do not roll out custom functionality when existing systems may already provide it.

The Blockchain Operator

The Blockchain Operator's areas of concern are in the deployment and operation of the blockchain network.

1. Deployment model: A blockchain network comprises of peers which hold and maintain the ledger, receive transactions from applications and other peers, validate transactions, and notify applications about the outcome of submitted transactions. Peers can run wherever it makes sense such as in a cloud computing environment, allowing a heterogeneous network to operate.

2. Consensus: Consensus is the process of maintaining a consistent view of the ledger. There are several consensus algorithms available today each with pros and cons, and the Blockchain Operator must select an algorithm that makes the most sense for the business network.

Table 5.2: *Examples of consensus mechanisms*

Consensus Method	Trade-offs	Example implementation
Proof Of Work (POW)	POW algorithms require validators to solve cryptographic puzzles to reach consensus and obtain a reward. POWs are generally employed in untrusted networks, use a high amount of energy as the overall computing power of the network grows, and are slow to confirm transactions.	Bitcoin, Ethereum
Proof Of Stake (POS)	POS algorithms require validators to hold currency in escrow and can be an order of magnitude more efficient than POW. POS algorithms are generally used in trustless networks with an intrinsic currency.	Nxt
Proof of Elapsed Time (PoET)	Nodes run PoET program in "trusted execution environment" (for example, Intel SGX) and waits a random amount of time (say, 10min). PoET creates an attested proof of elapsed time and is dependent on processor extensions to work.	Sawtooth Ledger

Practical Byzantine Fault Tolerance (PBFT) implementations	PBFT algorithms use the concept of a replicated state machine and voting by replicas for state changes. Some variants provide optimizations such as signing and encryption of messages exchanged between replicas and clients, reducing the size and number of messages exchanged, for the system to be practical in the face of Byzantine faults. PBFT algorithms require "3f+1" replicas to be able to tolerate "f" failing nodes.	Hyperledger Fabric v0.6
Transaction Ordering	The operating assumption for Hyperledger developers is that business blockchain networks operate in an environment of partial trust. In this implementation, the consensus approach is permissioned voting-based while a transaction Leader does ordering. Only in-sync replicas are voted as a leader. This approach is crash fault tolerant, and transaction finality happens in seconds, but this approach is not Byzantine fault tolerant which prevents the system from reaching agreement in case of malicious or faulty nodes.	Hyperledger Fabric v1.0

The Blockchain Architect

The Blockchain Architects are responsible with the development and operational concerns of the network including the business application, smart contract logic, integration with existing systems, security of the network, and the mechanism used to achieve consensus.

1. Enterprise Architecture considerations – before a blockchain project starts, the architects must examine business process to determine the suitability of blockchain for solving the problem. This evaluation also

determines the asset(s) traded on the blockchain, the attributes of those assets, any references to external data systems that may be necessary for smart contracts, and evaluation of privacy and confidentiality requirements. They identify the blockchain network member population along with the common goal of the network.

2. Business Considerations – Blockchain adds many dimensions to an application that is not present in other software projects. For example, who pays for the blockchain network? Where are the peers are hosted? What type of data is stored in the ledger? How shall the API call existing IT systems?

3. Technical Architecture considerations: The blockchain architects must consider the network membership model, peer design, the roles of the various nodes in the network, and policies for membership, confidentiality, and member onboarding. Some of these decisions may be encoded as smart contracts for the business network, so interlock with blockchain developers is necessary. The lifecycle of smart contracts should be well thought out in the modern Continuous Delivery fashion including testing, and a formal method for smart contract modification has to be established. The network topology must be well defined before implementation since permissioned blockchains do not operate in a trustless environment.

Blockchain Architects must arrive at architectural decisions for many non-functional requirements. The architectural decisions are trade-offs between several options and affect the performance of the overall blockchain solution. The typical areas of non-functional requirements that blockchain architects must wrestle with are in the areas.

- Security – The identity of the network members is known in permissioned networks, but good software architecture dictates the sharing of least amount of information without impact application performance. Careful consideration is necessary to share only required information about the assets traded on the network, and it requires a deep under-standing of confidentiality of transactions.

- Performance – The blockchain architects must weigh the latency and throughput of the blockchain network based on the deployment model against the transaction throughput expected by the network. The block-chain architects must develop a rollout plan with transaction projection for the full network at scale, along with policies to change consensus mechanism if the network may struggle to commit transactions.

- Resiliency – Blockchain may improve the overall resilience of the ap-plication due to the distributed deployment of the nodes (for example, if a ledger or node in the arrangement is inoperable or compromised, the other nodes can allow for the continued processing of transactions). However, the distribution of nodes may also increase latency. DLT ar-rangements characterized by a large number of distributed nodes may raise important questions related to governance and operational risk management.

5.7 Key Technical Decisions

There are several design decisions in any blockchain project that impact the overall architecture and can be very expensive to change at a later date. Such choices include:

1. Direct or Indirect participation: Within a consortium based blockchain network, a member organization may take part directly or indirectly. Direct participation is where a member organization "owns" a peer node. Indirect participation is where a member organization (usually a smaller org) uses services provided by a peer node via the access channels. Here, the peer node itself is "owned" by another organization. The master organization will interface with the blockchain network on behalf of the indirect participants. The indirect participant will reuse the peers and CA hosted by master organization. However, master

organization and consortium will need to consider any legal implications and potential liabilities that may arise (to master participant) due to actions of indirect participant on the network. This could cause concern from data privacy perspective since data for the indirect participant will be on the same channel with other indirect participants. If the master organization creates a channel for each indirect participant, this could lead to significant operational complexity and costs for the master organization. In addition, the need for isolating the UI, transactions and data between the indirect members might dictate need to segregate indirect participants at user interface level, front end application level or even create separate UIs

2. Key Management: Ensuring security of key management operations (generation, storage, and use of keys within cryptographic operations) within blockchain solutions. The choice here is to use a Hardware Security Module (HSM) or a custom solution. Good practice recommends HSM for secure key generation, storage and for performing crypto operations. Scaling out HSMs will cause significant cost and operational complexity. There may be alternative, custom-built solutions but are not preferred for production applications.

3. On-Chain vs. Off-Chain data storage: In some blockchain based solutions (such as KYC), there is a need to exchange documents, images, files, etc, associated with transaction data. The options here are to store data on blockchain or off-chain in a separate data store. Storing this data has the advantages of reduced development complexity since smart contracts will manage life cycle of object data along with life cycle of related data attributes it stores on chain. Data pertaining to the Object can be kept in sync more easily with other relevant data attributes since both live on the chain. Access controls can be applied for both the object and other data on the chain since they are enforced in a consistent manner. However, off-chain data storage has its own advantages too. If the associated data is stored in a ObjectStorage service in a cloud computing environment, it would be highly-available and more scalable. However, off-chain storage

increases complexity since the lifecycle of stored data has to be managed, access controls must be in place to ensure consistent operations, and they must give considerations to protect documents from malicious access.

4. Smart Contract Design: The decision to here is to determine the strategy for encapsulation of decision logic either in smart contract code or in an external system. Coding decision logic within smart contracts has the advantage that the solution can be developed without requiring an external decision management system, however, it may be too complex to manage and update the smart contracts if the business rules encoded in the smart contracts have to be changed frequently. The alternative is to externalize decision logic to an external rules engine such as IBM Operational Decision Manager (ODM). Externalizing of business offers business stakeholders the flexibility to change decision logic without having to open the smart contract code. It is easier to keep pace with market changes in fast-changing business environments. However, the drawback is that solutions like IBM ODM add to the overall cost of the project.

5. PII and GDPR: GDPR aims to give EU citizens and residents control of their personal data. Personal data in GDPR means "any information relating to an identified or identifiable natural person who can be identified, directly or indirectly, by reference to an identifier (e.g. name, identification number, location data, online identifier, one or more factors specific to the physical, physiological, genetic, mental, economic, cultural or social identity of that natural person)". The "right to erasure" has impacts blockchain solutions because blockchains are an "append only" system, so it is not possible to erase data stored in it and data immutability is a key and desired characteristic of such solutions. The options are to store personal data in a side database and delete them when needed (hard erasure), or store personal data on the blockchain but use cryptographic features to make personal data in the blockchain unreadable (soft erasure).

CHAPTER 6

DISRUPTIVE INNOVATION ENABLED BY BLOCKCHAIN

6.1 Identity

We are living in a world that is data-driven. Modern computer systems have collected approximately 20% of world's data in the past few years. In this digital and networked world, we have a counterpart in the form of a digital identity in cyberspace to represent an individual, organization or electronic device. Like its physical counterpart, digital identity comprises a set of attributes such as username and password, date of birth, and other user-supplied or derived attributes.

Identity plays a crucial role in our lives – from the moment we wake up and check email, consume news from either news aggregation websites or social media, to getting on a plane – identity governs every aspect of our lives even though we may not realize it. Further, the attributes linked to digital identity increase in number and sensitivity as the importance of the systems systems we interact with increases in association or impact, both in cyberspace and real life. For example, newsletters or messaging applications may only require an email address, while interaction with financial institutions may require additional attributes like social security number and date of birth.

Identity was a physical construct and the governments verified and issued official documentation such as a passport after verification of the information provided by citizens. However, about 1.5 billion people cannot establish their own identity to satisfy pre-requisites for getting a government issued ID which excludes them from property ownership, social protection, and even financial systems.

The need for trusted digital identity is increasing with the rise of smart-phones, which affects transaction volumes for identity-dependent transactions and customer expectations for omnichannel delivery. Other factors include the growing complexity of transactions involving different entities (where iden-tities may not be established offline for example, in cross-border payments) and increasing speed of financial or reputational damage (in case of security breaches).

Digital identity is a multi-layered, global issue. Each person has several digital clones (or representations) stored in data silos across every institution and organization with whom they have a relationship (for buying, selling, or renting of good and services). Each person had on average 25 online accounts that required a password in 2006, and the number of accounts we use is growing at 14, meaning it doubles every 5 years. Apart from the mind-boggling fact that this would mean we would have over 200 online accounts by 2020 secured by less than unique passwords per individual on average, this shows that our online identity is now as important as traditional, government-issued identity. Apart from the complexity of managing passwords, rapid digitization of the world economy is changing the way citizens think about their own identity:

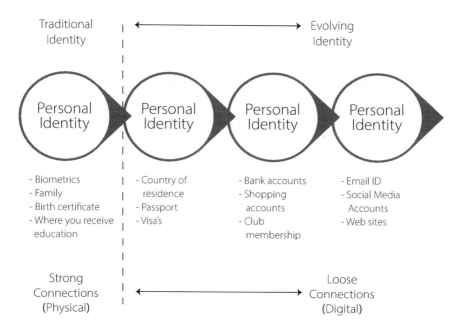

Figure 6.1: *Change in citizens' view of identity*

Our ideas of personal identities and who we are in the physical world tie us to physical, biological and sociological attributes we carry with ourselves. Some of these attributes are immutable – such as our biometric data. As the bulk of interactions move to the digital world, the connections between the evolving senses of identity are loose, and not may other identity aspects have all of an individual's data. The inherent identity attributes may not change (such as biometrics or family data), while accumulated (such as health records, bank accounts, club memberships) and assigned attributes may change over time (such as country of residence, passport number, visa numbers).

A robust online identity system must satisfy three attributes:

1. Security: It must protect the identity information, including all inherent, accumulated and assigned attributes from nefarious and unintentional disclosure.

2. Control: The owner of the identity (be it an individual, organization or a

digital entity) must be in control of who can see and access the attributes associated with the identity.

3. Portability: The identity owner must be able to port the identity attributes between solutions and not tied to any provider.

Let's also consider who's involved in the process of identity creation, protection and consumption:

Who's Involved	Their Needs
The citizen.	"I want to be in control of who can access each part of my personal information" "I don't want to enter information multiple times" "I want personal information held safely and securely"
The identity provider / validator issues the identification and validates important changes. Usually a government but can also be a bank.	"We need to offer quick and easy access to all services" "We need to reduce fraud and identity theft, and making online business safe and easy" "We need to increase revenue from credentials issuance, whilst protecting citizen privacy"
The *identity consumer* who provides goods and services to the citizen. An online retailer, government department, or bank.	"Getting a service from us needs to be quick, easy and painless" "We need better to understand, respect and serve the needs of our customers"

Table 6.1: *Identity creation, protection and consumption*

The Internet and the rise of e-commerce websites evolved our thinking and solutions for online identity. The solutions for online identity have evolved in four broad stages since the Internet:

1. Centralized – Most Internet identities are centralized, ie, owned and controlled by a single entity such as a website or a social network. This is non-transferable to external entities, resulting in proliferation of IDs and passwords we know.

2. Federated – Federation gives portability to identity, by enabling a user to sign into multiple services using the same credentials. Within a large organization, it may carry more complex credentials and ownership across applications. The most common examples are enterprise directories such as Microsoft Active Directory, or the use of Facebook and Google ID across several websites on the Internet. In this model, multiple, federated authorities keep administrative control of identity.

3. User-Centric – The idea behind user-centric identity is to build a 'persistent online identity' into the fabric of the next generation of the Internet or web 2.0. This effort, called Identity 2.0, led to the basis of the OpenID standard and formation of OpenID foundation. OpenID allows user authentication by a third-party service, enabling users to login into multiple unrelated without having separate username and passwords for each. However, some argue that OpenID is another form of central authority, and other implementations such as Facebook Connect have been launched, defeating the original user-centric idea of control.

4. Self-Sovereign – This is the final step in the evolution of online identity, and provides all three elements of security, control and portability. It turns identity owner and provider upside down – the identity owner becomes the provider and can own, control and manage their identity. The identity owner can see the attributes associated with their identity, reveal select attributes to a service provider, and can share the attributes with other providers to get a new service. Conventional approaches to identity have struggled with portability, and self-sovereign identity ushers in the post-silo, distributed world. Each organization can have a single connection to the collective network providing the identity layer, and access the identities and associated attributes via APIs.

There is a clear parallel in the evolution of blockchain and digital identity as shown in the figure below. The rise of blockchain technologies presents a unique opportunity to make self-sovereign, citizen-identity real:

Blockchain / Distributed Ledger

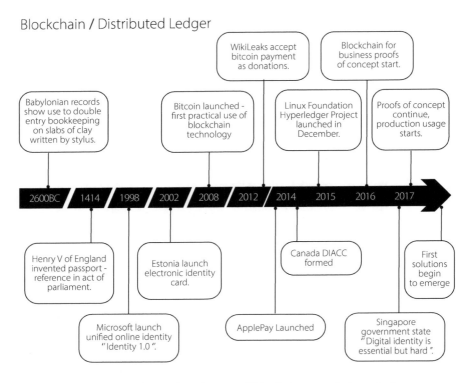

Figure 6.2: *Timeline of evolution of blockchain and digital identity*

Blockchain value in distributed identity network

Blockchain can develop a trust platform for decentralized, citizen-centric identity.

Using blockchain for an identity network differs from earlier approaches and makes in citizen-centric and even self-sovereign in following ways:

- The citizens (or identity providers) own and control their identity along with all associated attributes and assets attached to that identity.

- The identity information is stored on a distributed ledger provided shared with all participants.

- It does not rely on third parties for the creation of identity, or validation of transactions associated with an identity.

100

Blockchain Attribute	Value in establishing citizen-centric identity
Business Network	The business network is comprised of the participants in the digital identity ecosystem which includes identity providers (aka, citizens), identity consumers (public and private organizations such as banks, governments, retailers). There may optionally be other entities such as identity custodians and external validators for some use cases.
Smart Contracts	Smart Contracts are used to enforce the network's rules around sharing of identity information and associated attributes.
Consensus	Selected members of network validate identity and any changes to an identity.
Provenance	A complete audit trail (life journey) of citizen is stored on the blockchain thus providing full traceability across all interactions.
Immutability	The changes to identity are tamper proof, and can only be performed subject to the rules of the identity network.
Finality	One trusted view of holistic citizen identity that is indisputable.

Table 6.2: *Value of blockchain in distributed identity network*

The critical components of such a citizen-centric identity solution include smart contracts (to enforce transaction verification), libraries and tools for integration of the decentralized identity system into existing services, and an identity wallet which is usually a mobile application used to control the identity and sign attestations.

Another emerging design pattern is the rise of Identity Custodians – companies formed as part of a consortium between the participants identified in the table above which spans the citizens, identity providing companies (or Identity Custodians), and identity consumers who may be Identity Custodians.

The blockchain identity services landscape is still evolving, with both mature vendors and start-ups investing in developing general and special-purpose solutions.

- Several startups are looking for ways to expand in the space of blockchain across industries. For example, BlockVerify provides blockchain-based anti-counterfeit solutions in industries such as pharmaceuticals, luxury items, diamonds, etc. BlockAuth enables users to own and operate their own identity registrar that allows them to submit information for verification. Trunomi empowers customers to manage and safely share personal data, with consent and control especially to adhere with incoming new regulations such as General Data Protection Regulation in EU.

- Pure-play blockchain identity providers are developing solutions and growing via partnerships. For example, Netki provides open source and open standards-based digital identity solutions that allow financial service companies to meet their compliance requirements on both public and private blockchains. Shocard enables customers to create a self-certified digital identity based on a government-issued ID, storing encrypted and hashed identity information on the blockchain.

- Startups providing blockchain-based identity platform are focusing on enabling developers to build applications rapidly with easy to consume APIs. For example, BlockCypher is an infrastructure fabric provider for blockchain applications and its APIs enable developers to build & interact with applications for identity management, p2p payments, etc. Blockstack provides a decentralized DNS system running on top of Bitcoin, removes any trust points from the middle of the network by using blockchain, and provides services for identity, discovery, and storage.

- Mature platform providers such as Microsoft have partnered with Labs and ConsenSys to build an open-source blockchain based identity system that integrates the Bitcoin and Ethereum blockchains.

- Thought leaders that have written multiple reports on Blockchain in FSS but have yet to develop tangible solutions. Their work is enabling companies to realize the potential of Blockchain capabilities. Deloitte and

PwC have Identified Blockchain identity as a potentially valuable service and announced "Smart identity" and "Vulcan platform" respectively.

Adoption of blockchain for identity services is in its early stages – FSS companies are among the early adopters, but other industry applications are emerging.

- Russia's Alfa Bank collaborated with BlockNotary to release a mobile app called Potok to enable remote customer loan interviews and ID verification. The app holds loan interviews online, which speeds up the identification process. BlockNotary is a blockchain startup developing tools to solve problems related to compliance with KYC and AML requirements. BlockNotary's remote customer ID verification software and service allows banks or vendors to safely accept new customers without requiring them to come into an office by video recording them speaking a script and showing their state-issued ID, then timestamping that video on the blockchain.

- Capital One announced a partnership with blockchain vendor Gem and healthcare API vendor PokitDok to address healthcare claims management issues. The technology will control who can have access to data stored in disparate systems and when they should have that access. Capital One and Gem will also use data analytics developed along with healthcare API platform vendor PokitDok to build a new claims service that uses blockchain to track claims for medical clients and estimate patients' out-of-pocket healthcare costs. Gem's core product is GemOS, an abstraction layer designed to make blockchains useful for enterprise clients by connecting their existing software to shared ledgers, and it serves as a platform for managing data, identities and rules on a blockchain.

- BlockCypher and ShoCard have partnered to provide an identity management solution that is being used for passenger identities in travel and transportation by SITA. SITA is an IT and communication services provider to the global airline industry and owned by a broad network of air travel service providers. With ShoCard, SITA developed a mobile traveler app that acts as a mobile single travel token that enables airlines, airports, or governments to verify passengers anywhere in the world. BlockCypher allows companies to switch from one chain to another by providing the same APIs across blockchains since BlockCypher is blockchain agnostic.

Analysts project the market for digital identity applications of blockchain technology to grow out of its infancy at a CAGR of ~65% over the next five years, reaching $300M in 2021. Digital identity is the fastest growing segment of the blockchain technology market from 2016 to 2021 at ~12% of the total market. They expect the market for digital identity blockchain technology applications to grow most over the next five years, but Payments, Smart Contracts, and Documentation applications will remain the most significant segments.

6.2   Decentralized Applications (DApps)

A new paradigm of applications has emerged with the rise of Bitcoin and its open source, peer-to-peer network, cryptographic storage of records (blockchain), and the usage of tokens to power the network. Such applications represent a new software paradigm designed to exist on the Internet not controlled by any single entity.

A DApp must meet the following criteria:

1. The application must be open-source, and operate autonomously, with no entity controlling most its tokens. It must store its data and records of operation in a blockchain.

2. The application must generate tokens according to a standard algorithm, and distribute some or all of its tokens when it begins operating. These tokens must be necessary for using the application, and it should reward any contribution from users in the application's tokens.

3. The application may adapt its protocol in response to proposed improvements and market feedback, but a majority consensus must decide all changes.

By the above definition, Bitcoin is a DApp as is Ethereum. The Turing complete smart contracts in Ethereum have a way for development of Ethereum-based DApps such as the crowdsource predictions platform Gnosis, a system to reward good communication called SlackCoin, and blockchain based virtual nation that is altering the way we look at politics and how we govern ourselves called BitNation.

The DApps built on Ethereum are of the following types:

1. Infrastructure: DApps that provide wallets, exchanges, developer tools and frameworks.
2. Organizational Automation: DApps that provide automation of business processes within an organization.

The Ethereum white paper splits DApps into three types: apps that manage money, apps where money is involved (but also requires another piece), and apps in the "other" category, which includes voting and governance systems. If blockchains could do away with financial authorities, could it do the same for other companies and functions within the organizations? What if there was an organization where no single entity was in control, but it codified the rules and governance of the organization as a DApp? This most ambitious type of app led to a leaderless organization called DAO.

6.3 DAO

Imagine a self-driving car summoned via a mobile app. After dropping someone off the car uses its profits to refuel itself at a charging station. Apart from its initial setup, it does not require outside help to determine how to carry out its mission.

Mike Hearn is a former Bitcoin contributor who has conducted thought experiments of systems and organizations that do not require outside help after the initial setup. Mike described how Bitcoin could power leaderless organizations, in his idea of a Decentralized Autonomous Organization (DAO), which swirled around the Bitcoin community after its release in 2009.

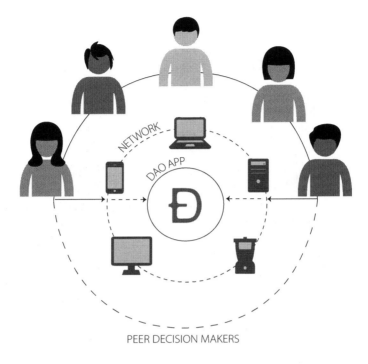

Figure 6.3: *Distributed Autonomous Organization (DAO)*

A whitepaper by Christoph Jentzsch, Chief Technology Officer of Slock.it, memorializes the concept of a DAO Entity. The White Paper describes "the first implementation of a [DAO Entity] individuals working together outside of a traditional corporate form can use code to automate organizational governance and decision. A registered corporate entity can also use it to automate formal governance rules in corporate bylaws or imposed by law." The whitepaper proposes an entity - a DAO Entity— that would use smart contracts to solve governance issues it described as inherent in traditional corporations. As described, a DAO Entity would supplant traditional mechanisms of corporate governance and management with a blockchain such that contractual terms are "formalized, automated and enforced using software."

The DAO was an autonomous organization created by Slock.it UG ("Slock.it"), a German corporation and Slock.it's co-founders, to operate as a for-profit entity that would create and hold a corpus of assets through the sale of DAO Tokens to investors, which assets would then fund "projects."

Because Ethereum backed the DAO, they could program complex business logic, such that the organization would be unstoppable once set in action. The blockchain would record all business transactions, and organizational changes on an immutable public ledger, authenticated and controlled by an extensive, decentralized network of computers. Further, since digital token-holding "investors" fund the organizations spawned by The DAO, each organization would in effect be managed by its investors!

The DAO was launched on April 30, 2016, at 10:00 am GMT/UTC (by several "anonymous" submissions associated with DAOhub, who executed the open source bytecode on the Ethereum blockchain), with a set funding or "creation" period of 28 days. The DAO went live with about USD 250m in funding breaking all crowdfunding records. However, after the minimum two weeks "debating" period, on June 17, 2016, The DAO's code was "exploited" by an unknown individual which used unintended behavior of the code's logic to rapidly drain the fund of millions of dollars' worth of tokens in a recursive call exploit. Slock.it, the leaders of the Ethereum platform, several cryptocurrency exchanges, and other informal technical leaders stepped in to stem the bleeding—shutting down "exits" through the exchanges to stop the draining of Ether, and launching counter-attacks. The codified governance structure – the key tenet of the DAO - broke down, and they disbanded the whole project, with a hard fork rolling back the "immutable" ledger.

While history records DAO as a failed experiment, the incredible potential of DAOs is alive and marching forward, as next sections would discuss.

6.4   Initial Coin Offerings (ICOs)

ICOs, or initial coin offerings (also known as 'token sale' or 'coin sale'), are a funding mechanism that has been used by blockchain start-ups over to kick-start platforms and projects built on a cryptographic token, like Ether, Golem,

Filecoin, or Storj. Instead of accepting some fund's money for equity stakes, these firms issue their digital currencies, or tokens, that anyone can buy in a crowdsale. Proceeds from the auction of these virtual shares help fund the businesses.

Enterprenerus use a Smart contract on the Ethereum platform to manage ICOs, such that the created tokens are distributed to participants with transparent parameters such as exchange rates. Investors send Ether or Bitcoin to this smart contract address and receive tokens. Owners of these tokens can trade them on secondary markets like cryptocurrency exchanges, and sometimes they are also the means by which users pay to use the platform or decentralized application (dApp).

The first ICO of note was the Mastercoin fundraising in the summer of 2013, which offered tokens on its platform for Bitcoin, raising 5,000 Bitcoins. In early 2014, Ethereum itself raised money to kick-start its blockchain platform, collecting over $18 million. One of the most notorious ICOs, and perhaps a forerunner for this current wave of fundraises, was the DAO, a decentralized venture fund build on Ethereum that raised $160 million of tokens.

ICOs have raised almost $1.3 billion in 2017 so far, while only about $358 million in traditional VC money went to blockchain startups over the same period. Browser startup Brave raised $34 million in 30 seconds, Ethereum-based enterprise management platform Aragon raised $25 million in about 20 minutes, and Bancor raised $140 million in a few hours. The rise of investment in ICOs was likely due to technological maturity and innovations like ERC20 standard in Ethereum, and financing of projects by selling cryptographic tokens had reached a critical mass over the previous three years through a series of sustained experimentation in 'alt-coins'.

The tokens offered in ICOs are of several types. **Asset** tokes represent ownership of an asset such as company, a piece of art. **Usage** tokens (also called 'intrinsic' or 'native') are transaction fees to write to a blockchain. **Work** tokes give owners permissions to contribute, govern and work on a blockchain. **Hybrid** tokens have properties of two or more tokens.

A typical pattern is for a startup to produce a white paper that describes their business model and technical approach. The white paper includes details about the functions that the tokens issued during the ICO will perform and the process of token creation. The tokens have a real added value – i.e., access to the network and used within the application itself. The contributors to the ICO sale get paid in tokens, which they can convert to fiat currency, and the goal of the token sale is to build the Network Effect.

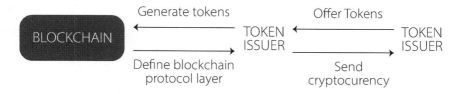

Figure 6.4: *Typical ICO process*

Distributed applications are at the core of ICOs. Startups develop an application (or application suite) which interacts with the smart contracts that enforce the rules around the token exchange and connect the application to a blockchain such as Ethereum.

The regulatory status of ICOs is uncertain since regulation has not kept up with the pace of development in the ICO space. From a regulatory standpoint, there is no definitive agreement on what tokens are. Users can use tokens to buy and sell goods and services like currencies; but like precious metals, tokens act as commodities or assets that store value or perform a function (such as, 'usage tokens'), and like equities and packaged investment products, tokens act as financial instruments.

- A ruling by the United States Securities and Exchange Commission con-cluded that some of the 'coins' offered in token sales are in fact securities and subject to the agency's regulation. A press release accompanying the report stated that 'The federal securities laws provide disclosure requirements and other important protections of which investors should be aware. The bulletin reminds investors of red flags of investment fraud, and that new technologies like blockchain may perpetrate investment schemes that may not comply with the federal securities laws'.

- According to the Swiss Financial Market Supervisory Authority FINMA, cryptocurrency business requires no special license, and they do not consider digital currencies securities but assets.

- The People's Bank of China issued a ban on ICOs on Sep 4, 2017. The Chinese authorities have concerns about several issues including illegal sale of tokens, illegal securities issuance, and illegal fundraising, financial fraud, pyramid schemes and other criminal activities.

6.5   Building blocks for a decentralized future

To build higher level decentralized systems, there must first be robust systems for storage, compute and bandwidth. Trent McConaghy defined the following classification helpful in scoping decentralized applications:

THE 3 ELEMENTS OF COMPUTING, DECENTRALIZED

STORAGE	PROCESING	COMMUNICATIONS
TOKEN STORAGE Bitcoin, Zcash, . *	STATEFUL BIZ LOGIC Ethereum, Lisk, Rchain, Eos, Tezos, .. Client-side compute (JS, Swift)	DATA TCP/IP, HTTP
FILE SYSTEM or BLOB IPFS/FileCoin, Eth Swarm, Storj, Sia, Tieron, LAFS	STATELESS BIZ LOGIC Crypto Conditions (e.g. BigchainDB) Bitshares, and all stateful biz logic	VALEU Interledger, Cosmos
DATABASE BigchainDB + IPDB, IOTA	HIGH PERF. COMPUTE TrueBit, Golem, iEx.ec, Nyriad, VMs, client-side compute	STATE PolkaDot, Aeternity

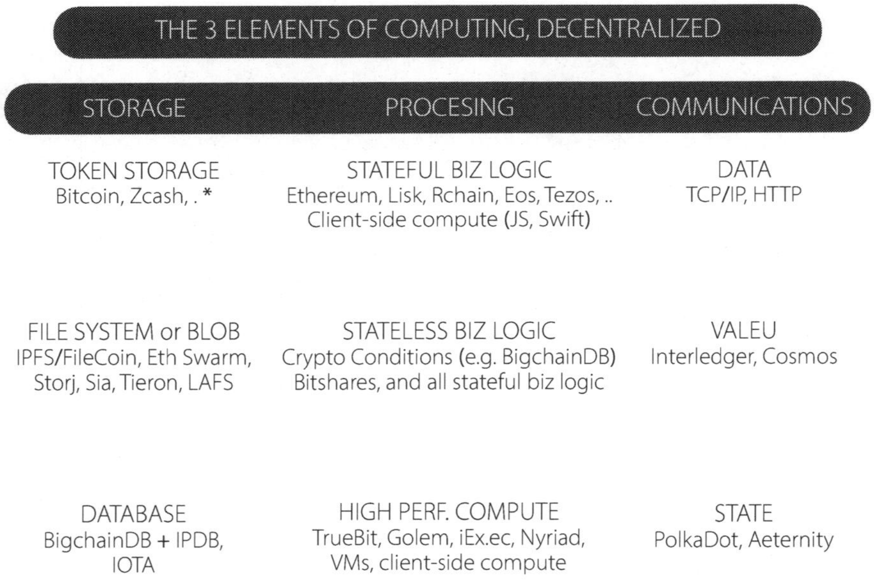

Figure 6.5: *Classification of decentralized applications*

- The Storage layer provides the ability to store assets of value (such as tokens, or other assets). It may store structured metadata about transactions or other characteristics of the assets in a decentralized database such as BigChainDB or CouchDB. Specialized filesystems such as IPFS may store large, multimedia files.

- The Processing element requires the ability to handle both stateless and stateful business logic, and the potential to support High-Performance Computing (HPC). Stateless business logic support is necessary to execute decentralized smart contracts. Stateful business logic is the arbitrary business logic that retains state internally but it also executes on the blockchain. It may require HPC support for use cases such as rendering, machine learning, and weather simulation.

- The Communications layer provides support for connecting business networks in three layers: transport layer to establish data interchange via protocols such as TCP/IP or HTTP, exchange of value (such as tokens or other assets) over the transport protocol while ensuring problems such as double-spend don't happen, and interchange of state information across business networks that may run on different blockchains.

6.6   Enterprise Implications of DApps

So how can enterprises enjoy the innovations and advantages of DApps?

1. Innovation framework / incentives: The ability of any organization to outperform the market is limited by its ability to take an idea from concept to reality. However, the nature of large organizations forces establishment of a typical innovation funnel, encouraging frontline employees to submit their ideas which are then voted, ranked, approved and funded by several layers of middle-management before formal development projects can begin. DApps enable massive collaboration across such innovation frameworks, where companies can issue tokens (to show voting or internal investment funds) on a private blockchain, and allow decentralized decision making across the enterprise. This enables large groups of like-minded individuals to decide on ideas they perceive

as most innovative, without interference from a middle-management chain limited by the innovator's dilemma.

2. Business Process Improvements – In existing organizational models, decision making process is slow and costly. DApps can simplify these processes, by recording everything on the blockchain, and automating all associated processes with smart contracts.

3. Strategic Decision Making – In all large organizations, few individuals on the corporate board at the top of the hierarchy make strategic decisions. Board members may have different and competing incentives that influence their decision making. DApps can make decisions removing extraneous influences with greater flexibility in arriving at a data-driven decision. The developers can configure DApps that all token holders can vote on decisions ranging from how to spend funds, who to hire, where to invest, etc. The voting process can be set by weight, ranked voting, and other configurations.

6.7   IoT and Blockchain

Internet Of Things (IoT) is about enabling everyday objects to connect, share data about that object, or the environment around it, and realize new insights, business innovations and enhancements to society. IoT devices differ from primitive sensors to sophisticated 'things'. For example, it could be a tiny, primitive sensor on floodplain monitoring river conditions and water levels which only produces kilobytes of data every day. Another extreme point of view for an IoT 'thing' is an airplane engine, which could generate terabytes of data in only a few hours of flight time. IoT solutions can represent these things or anything in between, a Car, Fridges, Freezers, Kettles, or buildings.

Consider IoT as digitalization of the physical world. IoT allows representation of the real world, its interactions, and behaviors in a digital format. With this digitalization, the potential benefits for business and society are immense. IoT with Blockchain can enrich those business networks who are enjoying Blockchain with a digital representation of the physical world. Gartner has predicted that by 2020 there will be over 8 billion connected IoT devices (excluding mobile devices such as Smart Phones and Tablets).

How does IoT work?

IoT is centered on events. Because of the vast number of things IoT represents, it makes more sense to consider events rather than requests. If we are talking about a smart kettle and we want to know when it has boiled, and there is a whole number of factors that may influence the time to boil the kettle including, time of day, the owner, the temperature in the building and so on. While they could make many assumptions on the observations and try to consider these factors, an alternative approach is to wait for an event to occur such as 'the kettle has boiled'. The IoT device can then send events, and it notifies any interested parties (other IoT devices, applications or systems) that subscribe when the events occur. A lightweight messaging protocol such MQTT is used for communication between IoT devices.

Why is IoT taking storm now?

Since the invention of MQTT, several applications and industry solutions for IoT have emerged. There is now a perfect storm of technologies and advancements that are allowing IoT to take hold.

- **Availability of cloud computing**: Cloud computing is cost-effective, scalable and elastic allowing companies to innovate and incubate ideas and grow them into enterprise solutions

- **Pervasive connectivity**: Connectivity in public buildings, offices, homes, towns, cities and even planes is commonplace and affordable. It has opened remote, disperse, and hostile environments to communication via innovations in low-power wide-area networks and mesh networks.

- **Analytics**: Accessibility to analytics tools is more available both regarding ease of use and affordability, helping to use all the IoT data to gain insights into innovation.

Why use IoT with Blockchain: What is the point?

Blockchain and IoT are both disruptive and emerging technologies. The combination of these two elements have a tremendous potential to change the prevalent modes of business and challenge the prejudges of society.

1. Blockchain brings trust to a business network, by sharing visibility, verification through consensus and a record for all of the time through immutability. For Blockchain to be of value to a business network, it still requires data inputs pertinent to the state change of the asset(s) transacted on the network. Business networks can receive data from existing systems or digitalized processes which they can share through Blockchain fabric. However, having accurate, reliable and secure representations of the physical world can be best achieved through the combination of IoT and blockchain.

2. Leveraging Blockchain for IoT data opens new ways of automating business processes among business partners without setting up a complicated and expensive centralized IT infrastructure. The data protection provided by Blockchain ensures faster resolution of breached contracts, stronger working relationships, and higher efficiency as partners learn they can rely on the information provided.

3. Reduce costs by removing overhead associated with middlemen and intermediaries. Leveraging blockchain for IoT data offers new ways to automate business processes in a business network without setting up an expensive centralized IT infrastructure. The mechanism of relying on intermediaries – lawyers, auditors, intermediaries – all have costs associated with them, they all contribute to additional layers of complexity. By embedding some of these capabilities digitally into smart contracts, some of these costs disappear from the system.

Example use cases

Use case 1: Improving workflow and real-time visibility on the status of shipments. Ninety percent of goods in global trade is carried by the ocean shipping industry each year. However, the complexity and sheer volume of the point to point communication across a loosely coupled web of land transportation, freight forwarders, customs brokers, governments, ports and ocean carriers, slows down the supply chain.

International trading parties require both improved workflow and better visibility. They estimate the costs associated with trade documentation processing and administration to be up to one-fifth the actual physical transportation costs. A single vessel can carry thousands of shipments, and on top of the costs to move the goods, the documentation to support it can be delayed, lost or misplaced, leading to further complications.

IBM and Maersk are addressing these problems using blockchain to exchange event data and handle document workflows. For example, in 2014, Maersk found that just a single shipment of refrigerated goods from East Africa to Europe can go through 30 people and organizations, including over 200 different interactions and communications among them.

Using blockchain technology to establish transparency among parties reduces fraud and errors, reduces the time products spend in the transit and shipping process, improves inventory management and reduce waste and cost.

Use case 2: Asset life-cycles and history. Every industry has an asset with a long life-cycle associated with complex business processes–mining equipment, tractors, and telecoms equipment–are types of critical assets which have long lifetimes – anywhere from 10 to 30 years. In most cases, the asset ownership changes over its lifetime. For example, an aircraft might have three or four owners. An aircraft has different parts replaced over its lifetime. Are the parts on an aircraft – over the full course of its life – with multiple owners genuine, in good working order, original and not counterfeit?

Using IoT, instrumentation and device authentication – right down to the part number – every part used in the airplane can have an indisputable provenance and history in an unalterable record on the blockchain. For the buyer, and the passenger of the aircraft, the safety, and reliability of that aircraft is traceable – and trustworthy.

Damage events are something an organization wants to know about. For aircraft, they track the number of hard landings as a vital indicator of the wear and tear on the aircraft. What if we could track and record the number of hard landings on a blockchain. We would have a higher trust in that aircraft's history.

The automotive industry is another area where blockchain can make a difference regarding parts and provenance – reducing the potential for counterfeit parts. Blockchain could have an enormous impact in any part-intensive industry – where the supply chain is vital to a manufacturing organization. Although a manufacturer might maintain a secure connection with its direct suppliers, the surrounding processes – for example, components delivered from site to site, may not be as airtight. It assumes trust along the supply chain unless there are signs of physical tampering, theft, or unexplained delays.

Determining provenance all along the way can help reduce counterfeit parts within the supply chain. The automotive industry buys thousands of parts (including sensors used in modern cars for proximity detection, lane deviation, and blind spot detection) from dozens of vendors. It's crucial to ensure these parts are genuine – with autonomous cars.

Blockchain minimizes reliance on blind trust while enabling real-time visibility into supply and demand – across the entire ecosystem. Using blockchain and IoT ensures each part receives its own unique identity as part of the supply chain.

Use case 3: Infrastructure management.　Infrastructure management is an exciting area because it's tough to enforce a service level agreement (SLA) on telecommunications partner. It's difficult because there is a tremendous amount of hand-offs between systems, involving a massive amount of data. In the telecommunications industry, FCAPS has become a proven approach to network management that works well in a centralized, single-provider environment.

The opportunity is that blockchain technology can also facilitate distributing FCAPS (fault, configuration, accounting, performance, security) capabilities across multiple administrative domains. By instrumenting and tracking each of these FCAPS on the blockchain – to track records across a distributed network where multiple suppliers and vendors take part in the business network – such as the telecommunications industry, it's possible to create and enforce service level agreements.

Infrastructure management with blockchain also applies to transportation infrastructure, and energy, or water networks – any business network where we depend on processes that span a broad ecosystem of partners and suppliers. Knowing the condition or key performance indicators of any infrastructure we work with is a compelling use case to explore because it guarantees we have transparency in the operation of the network using blockchain.

Use case 4: Guaranteeing the safety and reliability of the food supply chain. There's much complexity in the food supply chain – involving many interim processing steps. For instance, a farmer's produce might first enter a food processing facility, then move on to a distribution center. Each point in the chain has a one-step view up or back; there's no full view.

The process uses different methods, pretty much on paper – which means it's not fast and it is error-prone, and there's no visibility along the whole chain. There have been some obvious examples in the last few years ranging from spinach to peanuts. The time it takes for organizations like Walmart to react to something like an E.Coli outbreak is critically important. Sometimes it can take weeks to figure out the source of a problem – the food's origin, where along the way it became contaminated.

Using IoT sensors and blockchain, retail giant Walmart is hoping to address these issues – improving the speed, traceability, and trackability, using a trusted network along the blockchain.

6.8   Social Good and Humanitarian causes

The distributed and secure ledger enabled by blockchain is the perfect plat-form to short-circuit large organizations and harness it for providing relief in disaster-hit areas. They could apply the technology to disaster help, for instance, in settings where there's an urgent need to track services. Given the common problem of aid leakage—loss of the vast amount of subsidies along distribution—an agency could use a blockchain to record the distributed items and recipients. Blockchains could also provide proof of provenance for material goods—a ledger, for instance, of the travels of diamonds from the mining site to the point of sale. In another case, blockchains could record vaccine delivery in areas where health records are scarce.

Blockchain can also allow a person to create and control her identifying traces. This infrastructure, if done right, could act as a new source of authority for authenticating a person's existence, with implications ranging from education records to voting. Blockchains could create another form of acceptable ID, offering an alternative to state-issued social security numbers that required for many financial and record-related transactions.

Blockchain is promising for financial inclusion. The blockchain ledger can give someone long-term access to a record of established creditworthiness. For a person who lives in a place with poor access to banks, a blockchain could document her informal bartering transactions or micropayments. The technology would then establish alternative accreditation in parts of the world that don't have access to formal financial institutions.

The World Food Program (WFP) of United Nations experimented with blockchain in Azraq refugee camp in Jordan. Using biometric information including iris scans, they created a digital identity for the refugees stored on a private blockchain. The refugees received cryptocurrency vouchers and stored in their digital blockchain accounts for use at the supermarket within the camp equipped with an iris scanner. WFP tested the pilot for 10,000 refugees and used an Ethereum based private blockchain developed by Parity Technologies and Irisguard.

BanQu is a startup that uses blockchain to create a digital identity for poor communities to allow individuals to take part in the modern financial system. Using blockchain, BanQu aims to remove barriers to entering the global economy, which can reduce poverty among developing nations. Besides providing an identity for the banking process and state they can link systems, land and health as part of a more significant economic identity. So far, BanQu has created IDs for several hundred impoverished refugees in Kenya and is piloting a land mapping system with small farmers in Latin America.

Bankymoon is a South African startup that has launched a crowdfunding project to help African schools, powered by blockchain called Usizo. Bankymoon has installed smart utility meters in poor African schools to provide electricity and clean water. Using Bitcoin, a donor from anywhere in the world can donate to the utility meter linked to the individual school. By using blockchain, Bankymoon removed all middlemen reducing the overhead to fractions of a penny.

Limitations and Challenges

There are adoption barriers due to lack of knowledge and fear of new technology such as blockchain. For example, the WFP has decided not to go through with their original plan to expand the pilot to 100,000 by August. One of the main concerns among refugees was data privacy since they did not trust the blockchain system with their sensitive biometric information because they did not understand this new technology.

Cryptocurrencies provide a fast, transparent way to send money internationally with low fees, but criminals have also used them as a convenient way to transfer funds semi-anonymously. Many governments are skeptical of this technology because of the lack of regulation, and potential money laundering opportunities. With a few countries such as Bangladesh banning Bitcoin, government regulation on cryptocurrencies limits the usefulness of the technology for all.

Another major limitation is privacy. However, most privacy concerns come with implementing blockchain systems rather than the underlying technology its self. Public blockchains store all transactions online for the public to see. As a workaround, cryptocurrencies create a series of letters and numbers (known as a hash) that represent a user's account identity. So instead of the public being able to see every individual's transaction history, the public can only see the hashes sending money to other hashes. With private blockchains, the data access can be permission-based such that only individuals related to a transaction have access to that data, protecting their data from the public. Be-

119

cause most applications of blockchain deal with personal information, private blockchain solutions are more acceptable as implementations in real-world use cases. Regardless of these measures, some people do not trust this new technology with private data such as their identity or health records. For blockchain to become widespread, people need to either trust or understand it.

Future of Blockchain for Humanitarian Causes

The first step to making use of blockchain is beginning a dialogue. Understanding what blockchain is, its usage, and its limitations are critical to starting a conversation about its potential. If an organization sees an aspect that could benefit from blockchain, it is essential to investigate and learn from similar use cases. What has been done in the field, what type of blockchain would be most beneficial, and what were the limitations are all questions one should ask when considering the use of blockchain. There are many large corporations, including IBM and Microsoft, offering private blockchain platforms and tailored solutions for organizations and charities who have identified uses within their industry. Unless a solution requires large amounts of hardware, setting up a private blockchain is not expensive; most of the cost is on a monthly basis because many companies offer blockchain as a service. A public blockchain is less expensive to maintain because it cuts out the middleman but has privacy and scalability limitations.

One potential use of blockchain is developing a charity platform similar to the Bitgive use case. A blockchain is a powerful tool for donations because of three reasons: transparency, cost, and speed. Cases of fraudulent and inefficient charities have lowered the public's trust in non-profits. For example, in 2010 the Red Cross raised half a billion dollars to help Haiti rebuild after a devastating earthquake, but in reality, little money went to help Haitians, and they only built six houses. Charities wasted as much as 40% of the funds were on overhead charges according to an analysis by ProPublica.

By sending the money to the beneficiary, a blockchain charity platform could revolutionize the industry by increasing transparency and lowering overheads by eliminating middlemen. A blockchain system could send donations (using cryptocurrencies) in a matter of seconds, which is vital in emergencies. Such a system would work by transferring donated money to a cryptocurrency, sending the cryptocurrency to a beneficiaries digital account, who could convert it back to a fiat (government regulated) currency or needed goods. This system would need a point of sale at the end of the process, where the charity could perform the last step of transferring the donated cryptocurrency to fiat currency or practical goods. Because they store the whole process on the blockchain, patrons could track when and where their donations have gone, creating complete transparency.

The primary role of charities would be at the point of sale, providing a simple method for the beneficiaries to receive fiat currency or aid, which they can use. In controlled environments, such as a refugee camp, this is not a significant issue however it is more difficult in unconstrained environments, such as natural disaster relief. One solution is for charities to team up with local store chains like 7/11 to handle the point of sale, as blockchain remittance companies have done. Also, seeing the money reach the beneficiary through blockchain could increase the gratification associated with charity, increasing donations. It is important to note that such a blockchain system would focus on monetary donations because transferring money on a blockchain is more efficient than transferring other goods. By developing a donations platform, a wide variety of non-profits could make use without the need to alter the platform for each company. If a sizeable philanthropic organization could develop a platform, it would increase the public's trust in charity, increasing the donor base resulting in a revolutionary impact on global humanitarian aid.

6.9 The EU General Data Protection Regulation (GDPR)

GDPR, which took effect May 25, 2018, is arguably the most important change in data privacy regulation in 20 years. This regulation applies to all organizations established in the European Union (EU) that process personal information in that establishment and all organizations outside of the EU that process personal information on EU citizens when offering them goods and services or monitoring their behavior.

GDPR protects personal information and give citizens greater control over the information. GDPR applies to organizations operating within the EU, and also applies to organizations outside the EU who offer goods/services to EU individuals. If an organization infringes GDPR, they shall fine it according to the gravest infringement, and the fines can be 20 million Euros, or 4% of the worldwide annual revenue.

Under GDPR guidelines, individuals or employees are classified as Data Subjects, while organizations could either be Data Controllers, or Data Processors, or both. Data Subjects are all individuals about whom information is collected. Data Controller is the natural or legal person, public authority, or other body that determines the purpose and means of processing the personal information. Data Processor is the natural or legal person, public authority, or other body that processes personal information on behalf of the Data Controller. Data Processors do not determine the purpose or means of processing personal information. They must only process personal information in the way determined by the Data Controller.

GDPR defines special categories for the collected information about Data Subjects and any processing performed on it. Personal Data is any information relating to an identified or identifiable natural person that can be used to directly or indirectly identify an individual. "Special Category of Data" or SCD, is personal information that reveals a person's racial or ethnic origin, political opinions, religious or philosophical beliefs, trade union membership, health, sex life, or sexual orientation. It also includes genetic data or biometric data. It requires a higher level of protection.

Data Processors must provide sufficient guarantees they will implement measures to meet GDPR.

Data Subject's rights

The GDPR provides seven rights for Data Subjects. Data Controllers must comply with Data Subject's requests without undue delay and within one month of the receipt of the request.

1. Under the GDPR, Data Subjects may **get confirmation** whether a Data Controller is or is not processing their personal information, and **to get** the information without undue delay and within one month of receipt of the request.

2. Data Subjects have the right to **correct inaccurate**** personal information**.

3. Data Subjects have the right to request the **deletion or removal** of their personal information **where there is no compelling reason for its continued processing**. This right implies the secure deletion of personal information in a way they cannot restore it.

4. Data Subjects have the right to **object to** the processing based on legitimate interest or performing a task in the public interest or in the exercise of official authority, including profiling.

5. Data Subjects have the right to **block or suppress processing** of their personal information in certain circumstances.

6. Data Subjects have the right to **receive a copy** of their personal information in a **machine-readable format** , and to transfer their personal information from one Data Controller to another in a safe and secure way without hindrance to usability.

7. Data Subjects have the right **not to be subject** to a decision based on automated processing, including profiling, which produces a negative legal effect concerning or affecting them.

GDPR applied to Blockchain

GDPR assumes that Data Processor and Data Controllers would be easy to identify entities such as Google, Facebook, Amazon, and Apple, that control how citizens search, shop, and connect. The inherent assumption is that centralized entities have centralized data stores they could examine for the data they collect, and identify all sub-processors attached to it.

Blockchain and GDPR started with very different goals—creating a network without a central authority or trusted store, versus introducing data privacy laws. In most blockchain projects, eventually the need arises to share information with participants and at certain times (for example, during a transaction). Every organization that takes part in a business network becomes a Data Processor and has to be comply with GDPR. Every node that takes part in a blockchain network may be both a Data Processor and Data Controller, depending upon the transactions they perform. The decentralization made available by blockchain promises data sovereignty and control over their personal data to individuals (or participants in a network).

Personal data stored on blockchain

Depending on the use case, data stored on blockchain may be data related to an identified or identifiable natural person such as data related to individual behaviour. The data stored on the blockchain could be stored either in plain text, encrypted, or hashed.

1. Personal data stored in plain text on the blockchain falls under the purview of GDPR and must be addressed like plain text personal data stored in any other data store.

2. Encrypted data that someone can access with the correct keys is not irreversibly anonymized and may not qualify as adequate security measures 'baked in'.

3. GDPR may consider personal data that has been subject to a one-way hash as pseudo-anonymous, even though the one-way hash protects against reverse engineering of the data. This is because it may still be possible to link the hashed data with the Data Subject by examining other transaction properties.

From above, the conclusion is that the transactional data stored on the blockchain will be subject to GDPR regardless of how it is stored.

The Solution

One solution is to store all Personal Data off the chain, in an off-chain, mutable data storage. It stores only the proof of Personal Data on the blockchain with salted hashes linking the entry in blockchain to the Personal Data. In this approach, the Blockchain Operators can delete Personal Data without impacting network operation. A downside of this approach is that it defeats the fundamental tenets that blockchain provides – those of decentralization and security through resiliency. One can think the off-chain data store as an Oracle that all network peers call via an API.

The advantages of this approach are it helps meet many of the rights of Data Subjects.

1. Data Minimization: Blockchain is an immutable data which is append-only so it will only ever grow in any deployment. Every node stores copies of the data which conflicts with the GDPR mandate that states that personal data be 'collected for specified, explicit and legitimate purposes and not further processed in a manner incompatible with those purposes'. The above solution does not store personal data on the blockchain but in an off-chain data store minimizing its distribution. For example, it will store personal data in nodes where the organizations require it, minimizing its processing.

2. Right to amendment: GDPR states that personal data should be accurate and up to date. In the recommended solution, it stores personal data in off-chain data store which ensures there is only one copy of the data. It is not clear whether the typical blockchain approach of appending a new block to update the information in a previous block may not be acceptable.

3. Right to Access: Organizations can implement a simple API or a read-only node in the network which can provide citizens with adequate controls (such as private keys) to access their data.

4. Right to be Forgotten: Perhaps the most well-known right mandated by GDPR is the right to erasure. The traditional blockchain approach would be to append another record which invalidates information stored in a previous block, but it is not clear at the time of writing whether this would be acceptable. There are other legal issues around this (for example, right to be forgotten is not an absolute right, and that it requires the Data Controller takes into account available technology and the cost of implementation). Storage of personal data in an off-chain store is the only way of fulfilling this right.

6.10   Blockchain and AI

Artificial Intelligence involves a machine that can perform tasks that have characteristics of human intelligence. The coming together of blockchain and AI is on the cutting edge of innovation and sometimes touted as the holy grail to prevent deliberate tampering with labelled data used by AI systems.

Big data transformed AI because it gave AI the ability to gather and learn on mountains of data, which brought down the error rate in acceptable limits. Blockchain technology could transform AI too, in its own particular ways. Some applications of blockchains to AI are mundane, like audit trails on AI models. But most real-world AI works on large volumes of data, such as training on large datasets or high-throughput stream processing.

The benefits of blockchain and AI are:

1. The decentralized nature of blockchain may mean more participants, and more data, which may mean better models. data is often siloed, in this new world where data can be a moat. But blockchains encourage data sharing among traditional silos, if there is enough up-front benefit. The decentralized nature of blockchains encourages data sharing: it's less friction to share if no single entity controls the infrastructure where the data is being stored.

2. Decentralized and distributed blockchain network may provide more qualitative new data, and therefore models. Merging data from silos

doesn't provide just a better dataset, it also provides a new qualitative dataset.

3. Shared control of AI training data & learning models. One risk in developing models with a disperse team is the lack of trust on the contributor, training data, data labels, and learning models. A distributed network on the blockchain that crowd sources the wisdom of AI scientists from around the world yet provides granular control and audit trail reinforces trust in the generated models.

4. Immutability of the audit trail means the model's outputs and the data they have trained the models upon can be trusted. Microsoft had to shut down its twitter bot after twitter users taught it racism.

5. AI with blockchains unlock the possibility for AI DAOs. This is uncharted territory, but one can surmise an era which deep learning models could power a specialized DAO and automate tasks done by organizations with human supplied governance. For example, an AI DAO which owns the cars could operate the self-driving cars, or perhaps the cars own themselves, in a future where humans may rent services from such AI DAOs.

6. Enable AI marketplaces. AI requires building on previous efforts and algorithms, rather than each organization creating their models from scratch. Information sharing, and composition of higher value models based on prior work is crucial to advancement of AI. Most of the sharing is asymmetric and ensuring lawfulness of data and models is impossible. However, with blockchain one could create provenance trees that provide full audit trail of the models, training data sets, and model output. The producers of the models could monetize them, and consumers will build new models using existing ones.

The most famous example of blockchain and AI coming together is SingularityNET, which claims to be the world's first decentralized AI network.

SingularityNET uses AGI tokens to pay for AI related services and hopes to develop advanced general AI they can apply to any task.

Other examples of blockchain and AI implementations are platforms such as Namahe which aims to boost the efficiency of supply chain by integrating AI into supply chain processes. Numerai hedge fund uses its platform to crowd source market predictions based on machine learning and steer the hedge fund's direction.

IBM introduced a crypto anchor in 2018 which provide tamper-proof digital fingerprints, and can be embedded into products, or parts of products, and linked to the blockchain. These fingerprints can take many forms such as tiny computers or optical codes, but when they are tied to a blockchain, they represent a powerful means of proving a product's authenticity. For example, crypto-anchors can be embedded into an edible shade of magnetic ink, which can dye a malaria pill. The code could become active and visible from a drop of water letting a consumer know it is authentic and safe to consume.

This combination of AI and blockchain is in its infancy but holds tremendous promise.

CHAPTER 7

SMART CONTRACTS

7.1 Introduction

A Contract is an agreement with specific terms between two or more persons or entities in which there is a promise to do something in return for a valuable benefit known as consideration. According to The Free Dictionary, "a contract is an offer, an acceptance of that offer results in a meeting of the minds". Contracts which describe and enforce rules for trade and barter were in use in ancient times, and modern contract law is traceable from the industrial revolution. Centuries of trade has resulted in sophisticated paper-based contracts with supporting practices like contract law concerning with the rights and duties that arise from agreements.

The digital age has affected contracting practices. Digital contracting has existed for several decades and in various forms. For example, Electronic Data Interchange (EDI) used by large corporations to share data among themselves, data-oriented contracts which allow machines to take automatic actions based on events, and computable contracts which take the information expressed by data-oriented contracts and execute business logic to enforce the terms of the contract. A data-oriented contract may have some contractual conditions encoded in a computer language such as the expiration date and amount owned. A computable contract can take the information from a data-oriented contract and execute business logic to send an invoice for the final amount based on cash flows until that date.

Contracts evolving from electronic to data-oriented, and again to computable denotes a trend towards greater automation. Expressing contract terms as data is significant since it enables computer-based contracting abilities that bypass the pitfalls of parsing plain-text contracts either via lawyers or the use of natural-text processing capabilities.

7.2 What are Smart Contracts?

In 1996-97, Nick Szabo outlined the functional and technical requirements for contracts embedded in software and hardware in such a way as to make the breach of contract expensive. He labeled such contracts "Smart Contracts". According to his definition, a smart contract "facilitate all steps of the contracting process" and included the aspects of search, negotiation, commitment, performance, and adjudication. The visionary thinking was that hardware and software alone could handle the full lifecycle of activities related to a contract.

The general understanding of smart contracts evolved, with the rise of Bitcoin and its success in decentralized trusted financial transactions. In 2003, Mark Miller theorized Smart Contracts are "contracts as program code, where the terms of the contract are enforced by the logic of the program's execution." Richard Gendal-Brown stated that "A smart-contract is an event-driven, stateful, program which runs on a replicated, shared ledger and which can take custody of assets on that ledger." Vitalik Buterin's defined them as "a computer program that directly controls digital assets and which is run in such an environment that it can be trusted to execute faithfully."

Szabo's smart contract concept required no fancy technology. His primary example was that of the electronic mechanism in a vending machine which performs two critical functions: It directly enforces operation by taking in money and dispensing products, and second, it incorporates enough security to make the cost of a breach (breaking into the machine) exceed the potential reward.

Consider a standard employment agreement between an employee and employer. The employee agrees to work 40 hours per week, and the employer pays out the wages bi-monthly. If a vacation is longer than two weeks, the employeer deducts it from salary. Thus we can define an employment contract:

```
(1)  On PayDay
a.  Calculate  the  number  of  hours  worked  last  14  days;
(2)  Credit  into  an  employee  account
a.  numHours  *  hourlywage;
```

An employer could implement the above 'smart' contract by deploying it on an employment blockchain and sharing it with all employees and other entities (such as trade unions, insurance companies, Ministry of Labor, and so on). Execution of the contractual terms encoded in the contract is based upon an external event – in this case, passing time.

For a more complex example, consider a loan agreement between a Lender Bank ('Lender') and Borrower Corp ('Borrower'), under which the Lender extends credit in the principal amount of $1,000 to Borrower at 5% interest per annum, included in the payment structure. Under the terms of the agreement, the Borrower takes the loan on June 1, 2014, and will repay the loan in two annual installments of $550 due June 1, 2015, and the second payment of $525 due June 1, 2016. We can represent that:

```
PayByDate  =  Array  (01/06/2015,  01/06/2016);
InstallMents  =  Array  (550,  525);

OnPaymentReceived(payment,  installmentNumber)  {
  if  (payment  !=  installMents[installmentNumber])  {
   breachOnPayment(payment,installMents[installmentNumber]);
  }
  if  today.Date  >  PaybyDate[installmentNumber]  {
   breachOnTime(installmentNumber,  payByDate[installmentNumber])
     ;
  }
  If  today.Date  <  PayByDate[installmentNumber])  {
   Escrow  =  Escrow  —  payment;
    }
}
```

Extending the smart contract to act in case of breach of installment amount or late payment:

```
breachOnPayment (paymentMade, installMentAmount) {
 ACTION: Insufficient payment;
}
breachOnTime(installmentNumber, date) {
 ACTION: Payment Overdue
}
```

There may be a need to change the smart contract. For example, the borrower's ability to repay pre-agreed installments may have changed, or new legislation may require amending the smart contract:

```
amendContract {
 ACTION: Change PayByDate, InstallMents, <other>;
}
```

Last, there may be a need to void the contract – perhaps if the Borrower pays the entire amount early:

```
voidContract {
 ACTION: Terminate Contract;
}
```

Smart contracts are agreements codified and running on the blockchain. Blockchain lends itself to smart contracts with its ability to establish trust in transactions. A permissionless blockchain such as Bitcoin incentivizes miners to perform with honesty and rewards them in the form of bitcoins for both solving puzzles on a sliding level of difficulty. Validated transactions are charged a transaction reward, paid to the miner who solves the problem fastest. A permissioned blockchain has the capability to establish trust among distributed but known members. The pre-existing trust frees up computing resources for more complex, multi-party smart contracts.

In today's world, the legal enforcement of contracts is cumbersome, error-prone, and expensive. The critical capability that blockchain provides to smart contracts is the automatic enforcement of pre-agreed contract terms by computers that represent the parties in an immutable transaction.

Cost savings occur at every stage. The code that runs on the blockchain replaces the traditional judicial enforcement mechanism, interpreting contractual terms, contracting and negotiation resources required for each organization, and enforcement of the contractual terms. In this context, the distributed nature of blockchain becomes even more attractive because it decentralizes and democratizes trust.

Bitcoin protocol provided a straightforward scripting language to incorporate limited program logic in transactions. Ethereum expanded that idea by creating the Ethereum Virtual Machine (EVM) that runs a Turing complete stack-based language, opening the door to apply smart contracts running on blockchain to unlimited applications. Ethereum smart contracts are written using programming languages like Solidity and Serpent while Hyperledger Fabric uses languages like Golang and Javascript.

7.3   Smart Contracts and Blockchain

Smart contracts are fundamental to blockchain platforms. With smart contracts, users can apply secure rules in the processing of transactions. They can use them to perform automatic validation steps and encode conditions that in the past were on a signed physical contract.

Participants in a blockchain platform agree on the format of transaction data in the smart contracts, and on the rules that govern these transactions. This agreement involves an accurate expression of the rules, exploring all exceptions, and defining a framework for resolving disputes. It is an iterative process involving developers and business stakeholders.

The process also covers reviewing the rules, registering agreement between the parties, testing the rules on transaction data, simulating scenarios to understand their business impact, and storing them in a secure and transparent manner. Data models and business domain models, represented by the smart contracts, require the same attention. Governanace of the rules must be agreed upon by all parties: who can establish rules, can deploy rules, and the processes for changing the rules of the network.

Three considerations for smart contracts and blockchain:

- **Using a Turing-complete programing language prevents exhaustive validation of smart contracts.** Blockchain often implements use-cases of trading value. Smart contracts act as trading agents whose action has a profound impact, manipulating value on the platform, assets or crypto money. The logic embedded in them should be protected and their effect predictable. However, by definition, the formal validation of a program written with a Turing-complete programming language is a non-decidable problem. Although a Turing-complete language is convenient, using a less expressive language and runtime, like a rule engine able to execute production rules, might be a better option to take advantage of more opportunities to check the semantics of the contract and apply formal verification techniques. Trading expressivity against safety is something to consider when the code controls the value of assets exchanged over a business network.

- **Smart contracts are business logic that should be in the hands of business people, not developers.** Smart contracts encode the conditions of agreements created by the business partners who trade on the platform. The conditions are the business rules regulating the transactions. For exmaple, deciding whether all funds, or a fraction, will be transferred to the seller when the buyer receives the goods. These business rules are likely defined in business contracts agreed upon by all parties. The contractual logic is likely to be real logic, which is of some interest to the business stakeholders of the participants in the blockchain network. Lawyers, business executives, or even end-users are the likely consumer and instigators of this logic. A high-level language, business-friendly enough to involve business stakeholders, would be much better than logic buried in code which is understood and maintained by developers. The need here is very much the same as in business platforms implemented for decades before blockchain. Decision management software enables externalization of the decision logic and expresses it in high-level languages that business stakeholders can understand.

- **Management of the smart contract life-cycle is essential and should be under the control of carefully defined governance processes.** Any change to business logic, which can have a profound impact on the company operation, is usually extensively controlled by strict governance processes. Once again Decision Management has been positioned to solve this problem and provide an extensive feature set to define review processes and manage the overall life-cycle with the expected level of auditability. For instance, business partners will likely want to review the rules, negotiate them, maybe even vote on them. Ultimately, they want to overtly control the whole change process. In situations where governance of the business logic is critical, a new version of the contract must be strictly validated before deploying and activating it. Any impact to the business must be assessed. For example, running a simulation over a broad set of historical data. Because smart contracts are objects shared by business partners involved in trading, a collaboration between the partners to define, review, negotiate, and validate the contract clauses is mandatory.

To sum it up, Smart Contracts are a clever and powerful mechanism to automate the logic. There are still many questions about its legal foundation, life-cycle, and the governance.

7.4 Integration with an External Business Logic Layer

A simple approach in blockchain networks is to encode the business rules of network operation as smart contracts. However, the encoded business rules are not accessible to the parties. For example, new participants entering the business network require a lengthy review cycle and coordination between legal, business and development teams to ensure the terms encoded on the blockchain are well understand and agreed upon by all stakeholders.

Second, the smart contracts must be updated when the rules of the network change, which may require another cycle of review by all participants, testing, and deployment on the blockchain network. There may be several reviews with legal teams to ensure the smart contract code complies with terms agreed with the business stakeholders who may not be familiar with the implementation language used in smart contract code. Consider a scenario where a business network in the automotive industry uses blockchain to manage the lifecycle of a vehicle. The smart contract code must be updated to accommodate each change when regulations are updated around allowable pollutant limits from the exhaust, or there is a recall on vehicle parts, expiration of licenses or other litigation. The business network would grind to a halt as each change requires a lengthy, multi-party review of the terms encoded on the blockchain.

Therefore, smart contracts cannot purely be code, in the sense that developers think about code. Smart contracts must be expressed at a higher level of abstraction, using business terms of the domain. They should be precise and formal, without ambiguity, but still understandable by people. That's what business rules are. Business rules define an aspect of business and should assert business structure and control the behavior of the business. Therefore, one of the business logic layers could be a Decision Management Platform such as IBM's Operational Decision Manager (ODM) which provides a robust rules engine and interface for business owners to devise, change and maintain rules of operating the network.

Enterprises need to manage change at the ecosystem level. Because the network participants define the rules of the network, managing changes must be a team activity. Many collaborative processes surround a smart contract lifecycle, according to the governance defined by the business network. What is the review process? Do we vote for activating a new version of the contracts? What is the emergency process to turn off a flawed smart contract? Principles that the business rules technologies defined many years ago are even more crucial as blockchain brings the need to manage business intent at the ecosystem level.

Well defined smart contracts require a Decision Management Platform representing operational decisions, automated and governed as business assets, and handled by business stakeholders. Integrating blockchain with a decision management platform is a good idea because:

- When working with something new like blockchain, it's a good idea to use proven and reliable technologies like ODM's rule engine where possible.

- It puts the rules for value exchanges directly into the hands of the specialists who define them — the accountants, the auditors, the lawyers, the analysts, and so on — rather than burying it in the codebase of the blockchain application.

- The specialists can use Decision Center as a platform for collaboratively governing their rules. Often, agreeing on the rules is half the battle!

- Extracting the business rules and executing them in ODM's enterprise-class rule engine provides better responsiveness to changes: Update the rule, test it, and deploy the updated decision service — all without touching the code of the Smart Contract. From the code's point of view, it's still calling the same decision; but now it is processing transactions according to the updated rules.

7.5 Extending Smart Contracts with a Trusted Oracle

With transient information (e.g., an interest rate), how can we propogate the updated data to a smart contract? One possibility could be to delegate this responsibility to the client application: The client application retrieves the current interest rate and includes it in its payload to the smart contract. Why would the network trust the client application to provide information reliably and accurately? Instead of delegating this responsibility to the client application, a better option is to:

1. Delegate the processing to get volatile information to a third-party known as the Oracle.

2. Deterministically agree on the value to use for a transient piece of information.

For an Oracle to work in a blockchain network, it must meet the following conditions:

1. Multiple endorsers must be able to get the same answer from the Oracle to preserve the deterministic aspect of a smart contract.
2. Reliable connectivity must exist between the execution of a smart contract and the response from the Oracle.
3. The responses received from the Oracle must preserve data confidentiality.

The following diagram shows the architecture and sequence of events for leveraging an Oracle component from a multi-participant blockchain network:

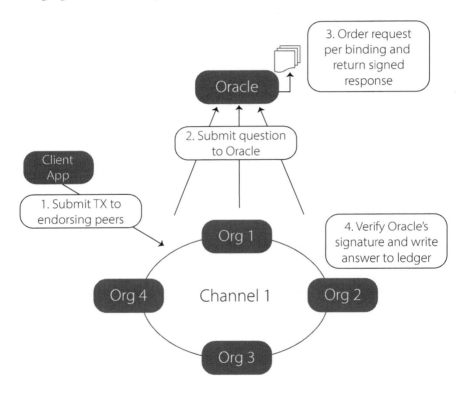

Figure 7.1: *Leveraging an Oracle in a blockchain network*

1. Client application submits the transaction to each organization that needs to endorse the transaction (as specified in the endorsement policy). Note that the client application is unaware the smart contract will delegate a portion of the execution to an external system.

2. Each endorsing peer in each organization will, in parallel, issue a request to the Oracle with sufficient information so the Oracle can correlate the various requests from the different endorsing peers.

3. The Oracle will use the certificates used to sign the transactions to correlate common requests and ensure consistency in the response. The Oracle may sign the response to avoid any potential tampering.

4. The endorser peers should be able to validate the signature of the Oracle. The ledger should preserve the signature and response data to provide auditability.

7.6   Emerging Application Architecture

Enterprise applications that now incorporate blockchain require an architecture suited to these modern applications. As I argued earlier, it is important to externalize the business logic in smart contracts from the actual smart contract code, which should handle data and event interchange with external systems.

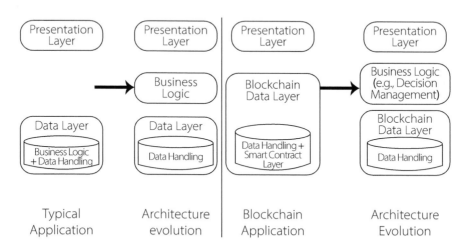

Figure 7.2: *Evolution of Blockchain Application Architectures*

Just as the application architectures evolved from business logic and data handling embedded in the data layer to externalizing of the business logic in a middleware layer, a similar evolution is happening for blockchain applications. Early blockchain applications inserted the business logic and data handling for manipulation of ledger data in the smart contracts. This is now evolving to the externalization of business logic in a separate layer. This separation ensures business owners can change the rules for asset interchange by using the language used in the business domain without worrying about technical implementation details and also enables scaling of the blockchain applications and providing independence on the underlying blockchain implementation.

7.7 The Vehicle Lifecycle example

To illustrate how an external decision management system such as IBM's Operational Decision Manager (ODM) can bring value to a blockchain network, consider the lifecycle of a vehicle. The following illustration shows the vehicle's lifecycle from manufacturing to recycling, through registration with the regulatory authority, and transfer of ownership when selling the vehicle, to eventual disposal.

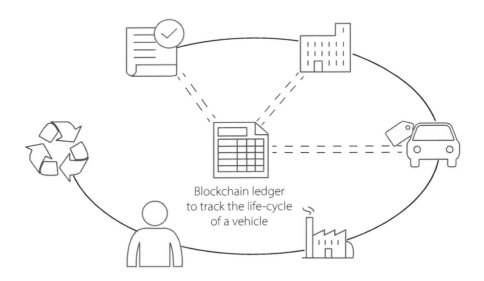

Figure 7.3: *Vehicle lifecycle blockchain network*

All parties in the business network have a trusted, distributed, source of truth about the history and ownership of a vehicle.

Describing the vehicle with the characteristics, such as its technical and commercial characteristics, owner identification, and insurance status is important.

Transactions related to a vehicle include the initial purchase order, manufacturing order, request for registration, and ownership transfer. Different rules govern these transactions at different stages of the vehicle lifecycle. Business rules likely apply to the sales process when purchasing the car from the car dealer. Change of ownership needs to comply with trade laws related to the vehicle, specific to each country. Participants want to detect fraudulent transactions on non-compliant vehicles or other tax evasion patterns.

Some of the transaction processing, embedded in smart contracts, is technical. Examples of processing include transforming data structures and creating, updating, and destroying assets. Other parts of the smart contract logic are much closer to the legal rules that govern the underlying contract between the parties or by the government regulator.

7.8   Topology of the Vehicle Blockchain Network

Figure 7.4 shows the typical architecture of a blockchain business network. Hyperledger Fabric is displayed here, but it could be any other blockchain. In this example, each peer node has its instance of the IBM ODM Rule Execution Server, which runs rules for all blockchain applications deployed on it.

A blockchain network runs on a set of nodes. Each node has a copy of the transaction ledger and assets, stored in a database, called world state in Hyperledeger Fabric terminology.

Inside a node, several processes implement the blockchain protocols and functions. A peer node in this topology is the set of operations required to handle the transactions on a blockchain node.

Isolated security schemes must protect business network nodes, so an instance of IBM ODM Rule Execution Server must be deployed for each peer

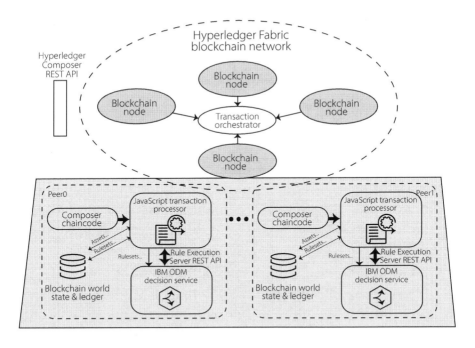

Figure 7.4: *Network topology for a vehicle blockchain network*

node. Multiple peer nodes make both the application and the rule execution capability highly available.

The lifecycle of an ownership transfer transaction

To illustrate how the blockchain application and IBM ODM work together, consider the case of a sell/buy transaction between two people.

To perform this business transaction, a system needs to publish a Vehicle-TransferTransaction call to the blockchain with all the information about the Vehicle, the seller, and the buyer.

Assume that the rules governing the transaction will check if it is fraudulent. The logic for these rules is complex and defined by experts. When someone discovers a new fraud pattern, the experts (business stakeholders) want to quickly change the rules to identify fraudulent transactions as soon as they are submitted to the blockchain.

The transaction goes through the journey shown in the following illustration:

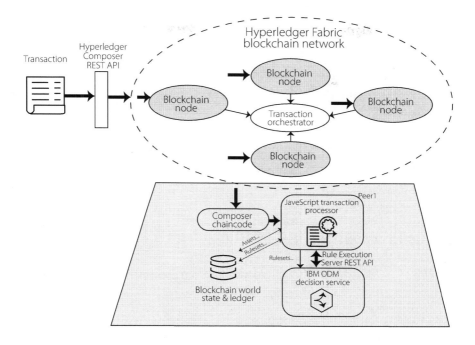

Figure 7.5: *Smart contract transaction processing flow*

- An external system, which could be a business process or an application, uses the REST API generated by Hyperledger Composer for this blockchain application to push a PrivateVehicleTransfer transaction.

- Hyperledger Fabric distributes the transaction to all nodes in the blockchain.

- Each peer node triggers the chaincode (smart contract) for this blockchain application to check the transaction and apply the logic implemented by the smart contract.

- Chaincode triggers the Hyperledger Composer transaction processor callback, defined in the blockchain application.

- Transaction processor (JavaScript code) makes an external REST call to the Rule Execution Server that holds the business rules in a decision service, passing the data necessary to take the decision.

- Business rules are applied to the transaction and executed by the rule engine.

- The rule engine sends the response back to the Hyperledger Composer callback.

- The callback performs actions according to the response, either rejecting the transaction or validating it, with extra information when it sees a suspicious transaction.

7.9 Smart Contract Challenges and Limitations

While there is little doubt about the ability of smart contracts to digitize trust through certainty of execution and creation of efficiency, it is important to realize there are limitations of smart contracts that do not always make for a seamless transition from the real-world into computer logic.

1. The distributed consensus capabilities of blockchains is a 'trustless' environment – i.e., the blockchain network creates and confirms the network truth without a trusted third party. Confusion arises when describing blockchain as a network where everything is trusted, including the smart contracts written on top of it. The consensus mechanisms enable the nodes to collectively agree on a shared truth, but that does not extend to the logic encoded in the smart contracts.

2. Another interpretation challenge with blockchain is that validation of transactions (to achieve consensus) is validation of smart contracts, or that such validation is legally indispensable. Blockchain provides evidence that a transaction has occurred after fulfilling the technical conditions encoded in a smart contract but it cannot establish the validity of the transaction in the legal sense. A transaction may be recorded in

the blockchain but the contract underlying such transfer may be legally invalid because, for example, one party lacked legal capacity, acted under duress or an illegality tainted the agreement. The transaction might have been an upfront payment but the counter performance may have failed or proved inadequate. "Putting a smart contract onto the blockchain" provides a record of its existence but a record need not always reflect reality - even if the record itself is trustworthy. The fact that the blockchain "validates" a transaction in a technical sense says nothing about the validity of transaction in the legal sense or about the validity of the smart contract the transaction forms part of.

3. The self-enforcement capability of automatic execution of smart contracts is sometimes interpreted as the elimination of human discretion on the side of the contracting parties or with the elimination of the need to seek judicial help. Self-enforcement of smart contracts in blockchain shields the smart contract from the vagaries of human discretion and protects the parties from breach, however, in a legal context, enforcement is associated with the state-sanctioned protection of the parties' economic interest in the performance of the contract. Courts enforce contracts by awarding damages for loss resulting from non- or defective performance, seeking to place the aggrieved party in the same position she would have been in had the contract been performed. Smart contracts equate enforceability with guaranteed performance, collapsing these two concepts.

4. The tamper-proof enforcement concept of smart contract can also be fraught with risks. "Tamper-proof" enforcement means that there is no stopping or changing a smart contract. If self-enforcement is to guarantee performance and if neither subsequent human intervention, nor a modification of the smart contract are possible, then its code must be perfect. Tamper-proof self-enforcing smart contracts may "shield" the transaction from the vagaries of human discretion but they introduce the risk of performance being affected by coding errors. An interesting result follows: as neither party can interfere with the operation of the smart

contract, breach is technically impossible – at least if breach is associated with an event related to or within the control of the parties. Multiple risk allocation scenarios are possible, depending they can attribute the coding error to one of the contracting parties or to a third party. If the parties used a smart contract created by a third party, there may also be a discrepancy between what the smart contract should do and what it actually does. The point is not that the parties may have trouble determining the actual functionality of the smart contract (as they can hire a specialist to do so) but it may be difficult to establish what takes precedence in the event the code of the smart contract does not match the agreement it embodies. They often make such decisions long after they have formed the contract as there may be a significant time-lag between the creation and implemention the contract.

5. The precision and digitization of trust encoded in smart contracts can create hidden costs. Unless there is well-defined and ongoing governance in permissioned networks, the only modifications made to smart contracts are previously encoded dormant options which may be alternatives. For example, consider a scenario where a supplier ends up sending lower-quality products to a buyer but will extend payment terms to non-standard 60 days to preserve the business relationship. If the original smart contract did not include this payment flexibility, it would not be feasible for the parties to arrive at such a settlement. The parties would be required to write a brand new smart contract, testing, integration, and roll out on the blockchain network for such a real-world scenario. Thus, it is not always possible to translate real-world reasonableness into digitized terms.

6. Some technical writings claim blockchains create a parallel transactional universe, or even their own jurisdiction, where the parties can transact outside of the legal system. There was a brief period of turmoil that followed the rise of the internet, and similar claims of the radical disintermediation as a natural consequence of its distributed nature. Contracts formed "in cyberspace" are now treated like all other contracts

and are subject to the same legal principles. Technical writings implying smart contracts and blockchains obviate the need for judicial protection overlook the simple fact that the lack of recourse to established legal institutions would incentivize not only fraudsters and hackers but also discourage the use of blockchains and smart contracts in financial transactions.

7. The difficulties of translating existing paper-based contracts into smart contracts is a non-trivial task. The viability of smart contracts hinges on the ability to express contractual obligations in code. There are multiple options: the smart contract can be a translation of an existing agreement, created in code from the outset or, drafted in natural language with subsequent encoding in mind. While only some contracts can or should be smart, most technical writings continue to extoll the ability of smart contracts to transform many types of contracts, including employment contracts, leases and mortgages. Parties can create their own smart contract or agree to use an existing smart contract created by somebody else. While there are no obstacles in creating one-off, customized smart contracts, economies of scale dictate that smart contracts take the form of generic programs and used on a mass-scale. One or more parties are unable to verify whether the code accurately reflects their agreement, or to determine how the smart contract will operate in practice. Given that the coders who create the smart contract cannot (or should not) decide on its commercial and legal aspects, there must be a document describing the substance of the agreement. Many smart contracts will originate as documents written in natural language that require subsequent translation into code. Lawyers and coders co-operating in the translation of legal documents into executable code can solve the problems of interpreting or supplementing contractual language. Despite such co-operation, neither the parties nor their lawyers can determine whether the code of the smart contract correctly reflects the original legal document. Such discrepancies are unsettling given that the smart contract cannot be stopped or amended once it starts self-enforcement.

To avoid the difficulties of translating legal language into code, smart contracts should be written in code from the outset. Contracts should be drafted with encoding in mind because most lawyers are unlikely to become programmers (just as most programmers are unlikely to become skilled lawyers).

7.10   Smart Contracts and Legal Issues

Given the vast sums of money raised through Initial Coin Offerings, the question of the legal status of the tokens issued in ICOs has drawn outsized attention. All securities offered and sold in the United States must be registered with the SEC or qualify for an exemption from the registration requirements under applicable law. Most ICO issuers have positioned their offering as "utility tokens"—providing purchasers with future access to the issuer's product or service. As a result, they have been offered without the benefit of registration or qualification for an exemption from registration. The SEC began studying blockchain in 2013 when it formed the Digital Currency Working Group (since renamed the Distributed Ledger Technology Working Group). It was not until the summer of 2017, however, that the SEC began to assert its authority to regulate ICOs directly. In a July 2017 report, the SEC declared that the DAO tokens issued by Slock.it were securities within the meaning of the Securities Act of 1933 and the Securities Exchange Act of 1934. This announcement was a "shot across the bow" by the SEC, establishing that ICOs could be within the regulatory scope of the SEC.

The SEC also clarified that in analyzing whether a token was a security, it would apply its traditional analysis based on a four-part test delineated by the Supreme Court in the 1946 SEC v. Howey3 decision. Whether a transaction is an "investment contract", and therefore included within the statutory definition of a security, Howey held that a transaction was an "investment contract" if:

(1) it is an investment of money,

(2) in a common enterprise,

(3) with an expectation of profits from the investment,

(4) where those profits are derived solely from the efforts of the promoters or third parties.

The SEC concluded that the DAO token met all four criteria and, as a result, was a security. The SEC's determination was not a surprise; the DAO tokens resembled equity shares in a company. However, because the DAO's was a relatively clear-cut case, it did little to resolve the security-versus-utility debate in the legal community. Since then, several SEC actions have focused on fraudulent ICOs.

In September, the SEC charged Maksim Zaslavskiy and his companies (REcoin Group Foundation and DRC World) with fraud in ICOs that were purportedly backed by investments in real estate and diamonds. In December 2017, the SEC froze the assets of PlexCrops. The SEC maintained that the company had promised unlikely returns, advertised a non-existent team of experts, and did not disclose the financial crimes of its founder. The complaint also alleged that the company violated the Securities Act of 1933 by undertaking an unregistered offering. The filing was the first by the SEC's Cyber Unit, which was formed in September 2017 to "focus the Enforcement Division's cyber-related expertise on misconduct involving distributed ledger technology and initial coin offerings, the spread of false information through electronic and social media, hacking and threats to trading platforms." While these cases sent a clear message to the market that the SEC would not tolerate fraud, again they did little to clarify the security-versus-utility divide.

In December 2017, the SEC stepped in to stop the ICO of Munchee, Inc. Funds raised by Munchee would be used to improve its existing app and recruit users to eventually buy advertisements, write reviews, sell food, and conduct other transactions using Munchee's MUN token. The Munchee white paper described how the MUN tokens would increase in value and highlighted the ability of MUN token holders to trade the tokens on the secondary market. The document even claimed, "as currently designed, the sale of MUN utility tokens does not pose a significant risk of implicating federal securities laws."

In the months since the DAO announcement, SEC Chairman Jay Clayton made several statements in his personal capacity in which he articulated his belief that most ICO tokens were securities. On the same day as the Munchee announcement, Clayton released a "Statement on Cryptocurrencies and Initial Coin Offerings." His statement was directed at two audiences— "Main Street" investors and market professionals (broker-dealers, investment advisers, exchanges, lawyers, and accountants). For Main Street investors, Clayton's statement contained a strongly worded warning to be wary of fraud and manipulation. He wrote: "As with any other type of potential investment, if a promoter guarantees returns, if an opportunity sounds too good to be true, or if you are pressured to act quickly, please exercise extreme caution and be aware of the risk that your investment may be lost." He highlighted a string of warnings that the SEC had issued to Main Street investors.

In his comments on market professionals, Clayton was even blunter: "A change in the structure of a securities offering does not change the fundamental point that when a security is being offered, our securities laws must be followed. Said another way, replacing a traditional corporate interest recorded in a central ledger with an enterprise interest recorded through a Blockchain entry on a distributed ledger may change the form of the transaction, but it does not change the substance."

Speaking before the Securities Regulation Institute on January 22, 2018, Clayton continued his critique of market professionals but focused almost exclusively on lawyers. Clayton zeroed in on the role of attorneys in this market and highlighted two areas where he felt they were falling short.

- There are ICOs where lawyers appear to be assisting issuers on structuring offerings "that have many of the key features of a securities offering but call it an 'ICO,' which sounds pretty close to an 'IPO.'" At the same time, these lawyers claim the offerings are not securities, and the tokens are issued without securities law compliance.

- In other ICOs, "lawyers appear to provide the 'it depends' equivocal advice, rather than counseling their clients that the product they are promoting likely is a security. Their clients then proceed with the ICO without complying with the securities laws because those clients are willing to take the risk."

He also criticized public companies trying to take advantage of the block-chain hype by announcing blockchain projects or "[changing] its name to something like 'Blockchain-R-Us.'" Leaving little doubt that stepped-up en-forcement was coming, Clayton added, "With respect to these two scenarios, I have instructed the SEC staff to be on high alert for approaches to ICOs that may be contrary to the spirit of our securities laws and the professional obligations of the U.S. securities bar."

Enforcement is not only at the federal level, but at the state level as well. On May 21, "Operation Cryptosweep" was announced. As part of this effort, regulators from across 40 jurisdictions in the US and Canada coordinated by the North American Securities Administrators Association (NASAA) initiated up to 70 investigations targeting ICOs.

Global Focus

Blockchain is on the radar of regulators all over the globe. In the wake of the DAO announcement, regulators in Canada, the United Kingdom, Hong Kong, Thailand, Switzerland, Australia, Gibraltar, and Singapore have issued similar announcements. Although the details varied by jurisdiction, in each case regulators clarified that ICOs were subject to the security regulations of their country, but also stressed that not all ICO tokens were necessarily securities. In the most extreme cases, South Korea and China banned ICOs—although with China there is a firm belief that the ban will be rolled back.

Class Action Lawsuits

Regulatory action is not the only risk faced by participants in the blockchain ecosystem. Attorneys have begun filing private actions on behalf of investors. In February 2016, a class action lawsuit was filed against the Project Investors, Inc. cryptocurrency exchange Cryptsy alleging that the defendant had stolen investors' money and fled to China. In August 2017, the court ruled that the defendant had to return 11,000 Bitcoins to investors, worth $30 million at the time. The Cryptsy case underscored one of the challenges in enforcing legal decisions in this space. The judgment listed the alphanumeric public keys of twelve cryptocurrency wallets where the stolen Bitcoins were stored. However, the corresponding private keys are needed to transfer the Bitcoins to plaintiffs. Due to the decentralized nature of blockchain, there is no central authority for the court to order to produce these keys. Autumn 2017 saw the first of what is likely to be many class action lawsuits related to ICOs. In early November, the first of at least four class action lawsuits were filed in connection with the $232 million Tezos ICO. The defendants in the cases are co-founders Arthur and Kathleen Breitman, Dynamic Ledger Solutions, which owns the rights to the underlying code, and the Tezos Foundation, a Swiss entity that was set up to carry out the raise. In the original Tezos complaint,24 only one of the claims is for the sale of unregistered securities. The remaining claims include two accusations of fraud and claims of false advertising and unfair competition under California state law. In December 2017, there were at least three additional ICO-related class action lawsuits filed. All alleged that the defendants had engaged in the issuance of unregistered securities.

Other legal issues

The rules of evidence at the state and federal levels govern the admissibility of blockchain records . Today in most jurisdictions, admitting blockchain evidence would require expert testimony. However, some states have passed legislation recognizing the admissibility or validity of blockchain-based records in specific contexts.

- Vermont passed legislation creating a presumption of admissibility for blockchain evidence subject to certain conditions and allowing for the creation of blockchain based limited liability companies;

- Delaware passed legislation allowing Delaware corporations to issue and trade shares on a blockchain platform;

- Arizona and Nevada passed legislation recognizing blockchain signatures and smart contracts. The Nevada legislation also blocks local government entities from taxing and licensing blockchain use.

- Wyoming passed extensive legislation providing among other things an exemption for "utility/consumer" tokens from securities and money transmission laws and allowing maintenance of corporate records of Wyoming entities via blockchain so long as electronic keys, network signatures, and digital receipts are used.

Jurisdiction

As lawsuits emerge in the blockchain space, many jurisdictional issues need to be addressed—questions such as:

- Which courts will have subject matter and personal jurisdiction over disputes?

- Which national laws will apply?

- Where are smart contracts deemed to be transacted?

- Who has jurisdiction over DAOs (decentralized autonomous organizations— organizations that are run through rules encoded in smart contracts)?

Are Smart Contracts Legally Binding?

Parties will inevitably dispute, and the courts must decide, whether these smart contracts are legally enforceable parts of the agreed-upon terms in the corresponding paper contracts. Although this is not necessarily the same situation as with blockchain contracts, it raises a similar issue: can contractual terms stored in an online source be incorporated by reference into the parties' contract? Courts found support for this in the Restatement (Second) of Contracts, which states that a contract "may consist of several writings if one of the writings is signed and the writings in the circumstances indicate that they relate to the same transaction." Eventually, courts will hold smart contracts to be legally binding and enforceable, and network participants (or Blockchain Architects & Operators) must place clear language in their paper contract that evinces their intent to incorporate the smart contract and to be bound by the terms of their terms and conditions governing sales.

There are many uncertainties surrounding the legal status of blockchain smart contracts. Incorporation by reference seems to offer a path to enforceability, but the ever-changing character of blockchain ledgers raises additional issues for the incorporation by reference approach. These questions will need to be answered by the courts when litigation arises from smart contracts unless resolved by legislation, most likely at the state level.

Will Smart Contracts be admissible as evidence?

The next issue with smart contracts is whether they will be admissible evidence if the courts determine that they are not part of parties' enforceable contracts. It seems likely that courts would admit smart contracts into evidence as business records, but what evidentiary weight will courts give smart contracts? Arguably, smart contracts are evidence of the contracting parties' course of performance or course of dealing. However, while the Uniform Commercial Code states that the express terms of a contract must be read consistently with the parties' course of performance or dealing where viable, the express terms of the parties' contract prevail where they conflict with the course of performance or dealing. If the courts do not find that smart contracts are part of an enforceable contract, they may likely attribute the same evidentiary weight to smart contracts as they do to other evidence of the parties' course of performance or course of dealing. Again, this is an area were state-level legislation may remove some of the uncertainty.

ENTERPRISE CONSIDERATIONS

What can enterprises do? What types of users and roles will develop and administer blockchain applications? Which blockchain application is right for your organization? How do you build a blockchain network? What makes a good blockchain use case? These are some of the questions addressed in this chapter.

8.1 Blockchain Network: Participants and Roles

Figure 8.1 illustrates a high-level architecture for a blockchain application where network members are interacting with the application. Each peer in the network has a copy of the ledger. In a permissioned blockchain, each member has permissions with distinct roles and, depending upon the consensus mechanism used in the blockchain network, each member may play a different role. For example, if Practical Byzantine Fault Tolerance (PBFT) is in use, some peers may act as validators that endorse a transaction to create a new version of the blockchain (i.e., the ledger).

Applications from each organization interact with the blockchain in one of several ways:

1. Use the blockchain provided API (such as REST API) to query or interact with the blockchain.

2. Send or receive data for events emitted by blockchain.

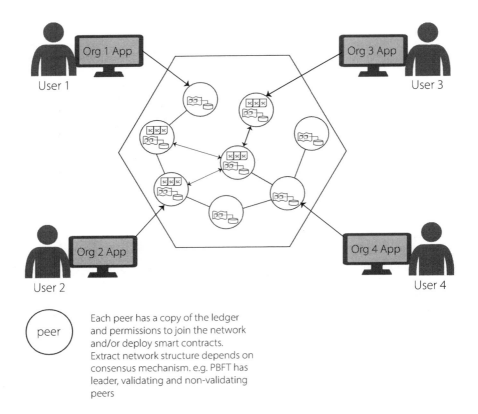

Each peer has a copy of the ledger and permissions to join the network and/or deploy smart contracts. Extract network structure depends on consensus mechanism. e.g. PBFT has leader, validating and non-validating peers

Figure 8.1: *Example blockchain network participants*

For any blockchain initiative, there are three scenarios which could lead creating a blockchain network:

1. **Founder Led** – An organization utilizes blockchain technology to solve a business problem. As the founder, this provides the organization complete control on the operating model of the solution and enables the Founder to invite partners to join the network. The Founder organization is responsible for development, governance, operation, and integration with existing systems.

2. **Consortium Led** – In this scenario, a consortium of enterprises who agree to solve a mutual business problem. One peer within the group

leads the effort for creating the consortium (for example, Walmart for food safety in the retail industry). It is like the Founder led initiative, except that members create a legal entity (i.e., the "consortium"). Consortiums are typically industry-specific (such as financial services or retail). The consortium members share the costs of operating the network.

3. **Partner Driven** – In this scenario, a startup or ISV develops a blockchain solution to solve a problem well known within an industry. As the solution gains traction both with venture capitalists and mass media, it motivates existing members of the industry to join the network. For example, Everledger developed a blockchain based solution for tracking of diamonds, and now diamond certification houses, law enforcement, and the online retail industry is accessing their blockchain network via APIs provided by Everledger.

The participants in every blockchain network play several roles:

• **Network Service Provider**: The Network Service Provider plays a vital role in a blockchain network. This is the network founder who takes the initiative of starting the blockchain network and defines the policies for membership, contract contracts, and any private channel communications. The Network Service Provider is also responsible for changes to the network. Additional capabilities are introduced as the network size grows. This helps to establish a democratic governance process which allows members to vote on accepting or rejecting changes.

• **Network Service Consumer**: The Network Service Consumers in a blockchain network operate an organization's peers and certificate authorities. They install and instantiate smart contracts, managing certificates for Business Service Consumers in their organization, monitoring network resources, and creating channels (following defined policies).

• **Business Service Provider**: The Business Service Providers develop the transaction logic (via smart contracts that run on the distributed peer network), business logic (via business applications and integration services that invoke transaction logic) and presentation logic (client applications run by end-users of the system).

- **Business Service Consumer**: The Business Service Consumers host the business logic for integration of existing systems with the blockchain network. An application server hosts the business logic either off-premises (e.g., on a Cloud) or on-premises, and connect via integration middleware (e.g., IBM Integration Bus).

- **End-User**: End-users run presentation logic on an appropriate device (for example, mobile application or desktop dashboard). There may be multiple end-user applications (often one per organization or user role). The value proposition to end-users is that the information they see is trustworthy, and may be unaware of blockchain back-end.

Figure 8.2 illustrates the various network members in a typical blockchain network:

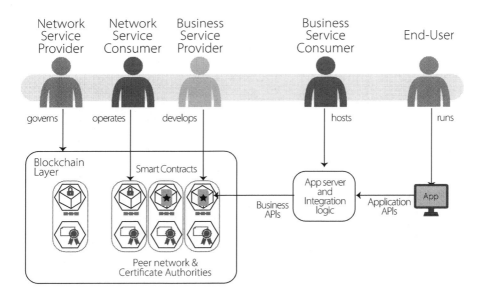

Figure 8.2: *Blockchain network participant roles*

For each blockchain network and project, each organization requires several user roles:

- **Blockchain Developer**: The role requires Blockchain Development skills with experience in building enterprise applications. The role is part of a software team that works on the business application of blockchain technology – focusing on the development of minimum viable products. The Blockchain developer roles and responsibilities include managing the application development while providing expertise in the full software development lifecycle, from concept and design to testing.

- **Blockchain Architect**: The role requires Blockchain Development skills with experience in building enterprise applications. The role is part of a software team that works on the business application of blockchain technology. The Blockchain architect roles and responsibilities include managing the application development while providing expertise in the full software development lifecycle, from concept and design to testing.

- **Blockchain Business Analyst**: The role requires a thorough understanding of IBM Blockchain plus relevant industry knowledge. The role is part of a software team that works on the business application of blockchain technology, and responsibilities include managing the application development while providing expertise in the full software development lifecycle, from concept and design to testing.

- **Blockchain Project Manager**: The role requires agile project management skills with an understanding of blockchain technology. The role is part of a software team that works on the business and technical application of blockchain technology.

8.2 Considerations for creating a blockchain network

First, someone must create the blockchain network, prioritizing the benefits of the network effect.

For any network to benefit from blockchain, it must address the following principles:

- **Mutual benefit**: Consider the automotive industry network discussed earlier, comprising of car manufacturer, parts suppliers, port authorities, shipping companies, car dealers, insurance companies, and car lessees. Each prospective participant will only join if they stand to gain from joining the network. For example, if insurance companies are asked to join the network, but they see no new value, they will be reluctant to join.

- **Network effect**: A network effect is the positive effect that an additional user of a good or service has on the value of that product to others. The idea is that each additional member that joins the network has a positive impact on the overall value of the network for all members. In the automotive network example, if the network has only one car manufacturer then the value received by other members may not be as high. For example, if that one car manufacturer ships cars only to a certain port then other port authorities may not find the network of value. However, if other car manufacturers join that ship cars to other ports around the world, then the combined value of network increases.

- **Design for a market**: Design the blockchain network at the level of a target market such that the network can recruit a majority of the companies operating in that market. If the network fails to recruit a majority of the market, then the network will fail to provide value to the participants. The target market could be a segment of the market in a geography where the network can recruit majority of companies. For the automotive network example, the target market may be the European car manufacturers, or port authorities in North America, or environmental protection agencies for the target car consumer market in say, Latin America.

- **Shared process optimization**: The final element of design for creating a blockchain network is identification of the shared business process between the market members that will be optimized via blockchain. It is not enough to simply recruit a majority of members within a market if processes for interchange of asset lifecycle remain the same. For example, the automotive network members require information about recalls for car parts deemed deficient post-sales and need a mechanism for all car manufacturers to utilize that information. A well designed blockchain network will provide a mechanism for all car manufacturers, car dealers, buyers, and lessees, to obtain that information quickly and with a high degree of accuracy.

8.3   Do you need a blockchain?

Most blockchain platforms are under development and rapidly approach maturity. Most enterprises are embarking on proof of concepts (or First Projects) to learn about the technology, impact to existing systems, resources they need to acquire, and how to create blockchain networks. It can be tempting to apply emerging technology to solve a business problem where existing technologies may suffice.

The flowchart in figure 8.3 provides a simple decision tree to help organizations decide whether they require blockchain for their use case.

Using a blockchain typically falls under the following scenarios:

1. Establishing trust among parties without an intermediary, such that no one party has more control over the operation of the blockchain network than another. Any modifications, deletions or updates can only be made by arriving at a consensus which ensures the immutability of contracts.

2. The use of smart contracts to enforce all parties to follow the same rules and achieve superior security over traditional contract law. Smart contracts also reduce the transaction costs of contracting.

3. changes are immediately broadcast to all members, which improves transparency to all network participants.

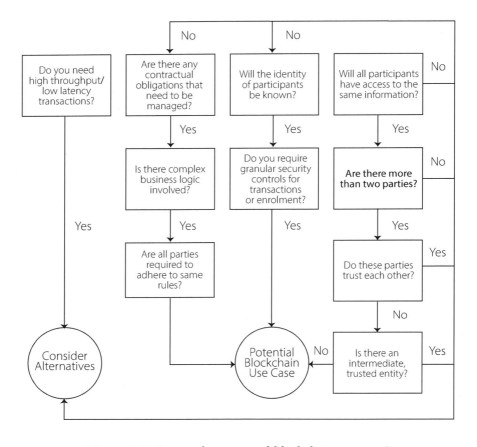

Figure 8.3: *Do you have a good blockchain use case?*

4. Only known members (who may all agree to use an enrollment provider) receive permissioned access and ensure an audit trail of all interactions among network participants.

8.4 Which blockchain is right for you?

There are several permissioned blockchains now available, or under development, vying for the attention of enterprises such as Hyperledger, Stellar, Ripple, Quorum, and Enterprise Ethereum.

It can get very confusing to pick a blockchain technology to address a specific business case due to the differences in use cases. Other factors to consider are the capability to hold asset state that is more complex than just cryptocurrency, skills to write smart contracts, and whether there are any vulnerabilities in how the smart contracts are being written based on dependence on timestamps or transaction ordering, and so on.

Below is a framework that can assess whether blockchain is a good fit for your organization.

8.5 Business Oriented Blockchain Evaluation Framework

Someone should consider the following criteria when determining which enterprise blockchain is right for your use case:

1. **Maturity** – Determined from the actual implementation results. Since the actual introduction of permissioned blockchains is very new, it is difficult to evaluate it rigorously. One approach is to evaluate a blockchain platform made up of existing technologies (such as cryptographic techniques, P2P protocol, ledger database, etc.) and new technologies (including the consensus algorithms used), and review the implementations of that blockchain platform in first projects or Proof of Concepts projects.

2. **Confidentiality** – Does the blockchain provide a mechanism for conducting a private and confidential transaction between two or more network members? What levels of identity and security are provided to members taking part in the network and in transactions? How are identities handled, secured and shared?

3. **Security** – What is the cryptographic architecture used? What is the protocol design? What capabilities are available to secure transaction data? How can identity management integrate with existing enterprise directory systems?

4. **Modularity** – Is it possible to replace some components of the blockchain platform with more appropriate implementations for a use case? If the blockchain platform uses a particular consensus mechanism, can it be replaced with another? Could the underlying database used to store the shared ledger be replaced (perhaps with one that may allow for faster querying)?

5. **Interoperability** – How can the blockchain platform integrate with other, existing enterprise systems? How about other blockchain platforms? What type of API interface is available?

6. **Governance** – Is there a defined and published governance process that shows how to make changes to the platform's source code? Is there a publicly available community that discusses vulnerabilities, shortcomings and other limitations in the platform? Can you contribute to improving the platform?

7. **Developer tools** – What type of developer toolkits are available to simulate and build blockchain networks? Are there any SDK's available for building, testing and releasing smart contracts?

8. **Scalability** – How scalable is the blockchain? Are there any limitations to block size? Is there any performance degradation as the size of the ledger increases? How long does it take for block confirmation?

9. **Industry Support** – What is the availability of resources, services, and entities that can help in implementing a blockchain project? Are there any readily available guides or cookbooks where others have documented their experiences with the platform?

Based on the above checklist, here's a handy table comparing some of the most widely used blockchain platforms:

Table 8.1: *Comparison of blockchain platforms*

Criteria	Hyperledger Fabric	Ethereum	Quorum	Corda
Maturity	First Hyperledger project to graduate to General Availability with multiple production networks	Limited POC implementation of mainnet forks	Developer sandbox only	Limited to R3 Consortium and Financial Services. Developer sandbox
Confidentiality	Partitioned execution, channels, and permissioned membership	Only possible through forks of the mainnet	All nodes are aware of the existence of transactions	Supported through "flow" logic structure
Security	Internal and external security review FIPS 4+ and HSMs SSC protect entire blockchain stack	No data encryption or channel partition	Private transactions, limited confidentiality	Intel SGX chips only protect verification portion of blockchain
Modularity	Pluggable consensus, database, and membership	None	Pluggable, supports QuorumChain and RAFT-based consensus	Modular data store and some programmable modularity through flows
Interoperability	Designed to integrate with external blockchain fabrics Backwards compatible	Interoperability dependent on third-party extensions	Unclear	Supports interoperability
Governance	Linux Foundation's Hyperledger Project	Ethereum Foundation drives development	Developed internally at JPMC	Developed internally at R3, no governance structure for open-source code
Developer tools	Fabric Composer free to use for developers	Only available through third parties	Cakeshop	None – written in Kotlin, a very limited programming language
Scalability	Designed for consortium deployment with high throughput	Designed for public network, limited by proof of work consensus	Design for consortium deployment, expected to reach high throughput	Potential for nodes to get out of sync at scale as a result of non-deterministic execution
Industry	Cross-industry	Cross-industry	Financial Services, aiming to become multipurpose	Financial Services

8.6   ROI & Monetization of Blockchain network

When large enterprises establish or join a blockchain network, how do they justify their investment and expect any return?

The ROI for a blockchain project comes from:

- Reducing the cost of networking – Network effects are a phenomenon whereby the value to the user or consumer of a product or service increases as its user base grows. Facebook, for example, is more compelling to potential users (including Harvard undergraduates) today than it was when only Harvard undergraduates could use it. When thinking of the Return on Investment (ROI) of blockchain network, keep in mind Metcalfe's law: The value of a telecommunications network is proportional to the square of the number of connected users of the system (n^2). With permissioned networks, the larger the network, the better lower the cost of adding new assets (for tracking and transactions), onboarding new members, or compliance to new regulations (since all participants can pool in costs to adhere to new regulations).

- Process efficiencies – A well-defined blockchain network can provide 20% to 30% productivity improvements by providing transparency, reduction in delays or trivial disputes. IBM Global Financing improved the efficiency of their commercial financing business by sharing data on a distributed ledger, and reduced the average time taken to resolve disputes from 44 days to 10 days. Walmart has improved the time taken to identify the source of a commodity in their retail supply from 2 weeks to almost instantly.

- Increased trust - Small farmers grow most of the world's coffee, many of whom depend on family labor and unreliable income—often less than $2 a day. 25 million of these farmers produce an astounding four-fifths of the world's total coffee supply. A startup called Bext Holdings Inc. is using blockchain to improve the upstream supply chains of key commodities starting with coffee. Bext has built a mobile robot which is sensor-laden to sort, weigh, and assess the quality of each coffee cherry plucked on a plantation. The robots analyze and grade the fruit based on its condition (riper, larger cherries generally fetch a higher price). They make the resulting data (weight, grade, and other specs) visible to buyers who then bid on the beans via a mobile app.

- New Business Opportunities - About 8 million tons of plastic go into our oceans every single year. The problem has greatly accelerated within the past few decades as the amount of plastic in the oceans continues to grow. But what if a piece of plastic was worth the right price? The result is the elimination of plastic litter, and the scavenged plastic can be exchanged for other goods. Plastic Bank aims both to clean up the ocean and to lift millions out of poverty across the globe by turning citizens in the world's poorest countries into recycling entrepreneurs. Plastic Bank realized that everyone—even families in disadvantaged areas—had mobile phones that could handle digital transactions and collect digital credits -plastic waste as a currency for change -that is safe on blockchain to help lift people out of poverty and keep plastic out of the ocean. PB sells the social plastic collected & recycled to brands to use as ethically sourced plastic in their products

8.7 Blockchain Governance

Public blockchains promise to transform the way economies are organized. They would achieve this by elimination of centralized third parties used to provide trust. There are already blockchain solutions in place that are solving the problem of cooperation – ie, establishing trust without a third party by codifying the rules of engagement as Smart Contracts such as the ones used by Slock.it to automate renting of rooms on Airbnb, or renting of cars, and unlocking of other physical assets in the real world. However the rules of how the blockchains operate, how the smart contracts are written, managed and updated, and the changes that are made to the blockchain infrastructure, can sometimes be unclear.

For example, in Bitcoin, the earlier protocol rules were developed by the person acting on the pseudonym of Satoshi Nakamoto and thereafter managed by a small team of core developers. Bitcoin Core has a large open source developer community and many more who contribute in other ways (such as research, peer reviews, etc.) and thus there is an arcane form of governance around bitcoin. The human element has not been eliminated, and the rancor between various stakeholders such as miners and some technology companies that contribute to bitcoin development has led to several controversies: for example, the debates over Segregated Witness for scaling of the Bitcoin Lightning Network, and the block size increase problem. The sometimes conflicting interests of the stakeholders have resulted in "warfare" on social media and other discussion forums.

Regardless of the promise of the technology, the human aspect of governance cannot be ignored. This brings us to an interesting point – we need formal governance which is somewhat centralized by nature, in order to deliver on the promise a decentralized world. In other words, this is the paradox proposed by Vili Lehdonvirta – once you address the problem of governance, you no longer need blockchain.

The paradox in permissionless blockchains is as much as (or no more than) the paradox of trust in existing intermediaries in today's business systems – the very same intermediaries that were culpable in the financial crisis in 2008 and were all bailed out. Other blockchains such as Ethereum already have well-defined governance to ensure that there is full visibility and community-based agreement on changes in the core code.

The World Economic Forum has published a more holistic document that provides Strategic Blockchain Governance Guidance at three levels and in seven Global Solution Networks as depicted in figure 8.4 below.

The WEF posits that "Governance means stewardship, not government or regulation" – a view that is indeed required in permissioned blockchains. No blockchain solution can be successful unless there is a clearly defined, published and accessible governance process.

For solution built on permissioned blockchains, following considerations must be taken into account to develop a governance framework:

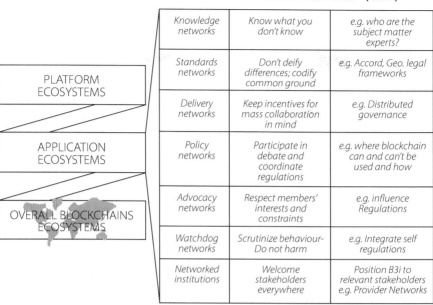

"Global Solution Networks "(GSN)

Knowledge networks	Know what you don't know	e.g. who are the subject matter experts?
Standards networks	Don't deify differences; codify common ground	e.g. Accord, Geo. legal frameworks
Delivery networks	Keep incentives for mass collaboration in mind	e.g. Distributed governance
Policy networks	Participate in debate and coordinate regulations	e.g. where blockchain can and can't be used and how
Advocacy networks	Respect members' interests and constraints	e.g. influence Regulations
Watchdog networks	Scrutinize behaviour- Do not harm	e.g. Integrate self regulations
Networked institutions	Welcome stakeholders everywhere	Position B3i to relevant stakeholders e.g. Provider Networks

PLATFORM ECOSYSTEMS

APPLICATION ECOSYSTEMS

OVERALL BLOCKCHAINS ECOSYSTEMS

Figure 8.4: *World Economic Forum: Strategic Blockchain Governance Guidance*

- Agreement on a shared and automated process on blockchain – What component is being automated? How is it automated? Where is it being hosted? How will it integrate with all members? What is the member participation/endorsement mechanism?

- Membership management – How to invite members? Verify identity? Announce new members (discovery)? Membership approval, denial, and revocation process?

- Network operation & fee management – How are new nodes deployed? How do new member nodes affect the network (if at all)? How to setup fees? How are they collected?

- Change management – Changes to the membership rules? Smart contract updates? Release management?

- Dispute resolution – What is the framework for disputes? How is it tied to smart contracts? How are disputes escalated & to whom?

- Network regulation – Who regulates the network? How is a decision agreed upon?

Figure 8.5 below illustrates an example blockchain governance framework:

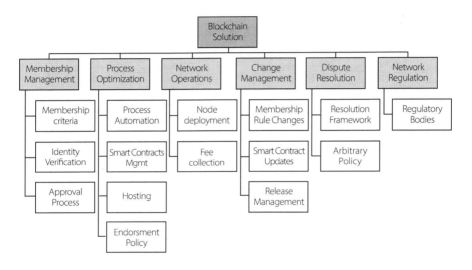

Figure 8.5: *Blockchain Network Governance Model*

8.8   What can enterprises do?

1. Find specific opportunities or use cases: Blockchain is a team sport that requires involvement not only from within your company but also from your business partners and clients. In three recent surveys by the IBM Institute of Business Value of those surveyed, 14 percent of government institutions, 14 percent of financial markets institutions and 16 percent of healthcare respondents, all plan to have blockchain in production at scale by the end of this year. So how will businesses get there? The answer lies within one word: collaboration. No one person or business controls blockchain technology, and no one person or business can or

should develop all of the promising distributed ledger applications that can ultimately create the "Internet of Transactions". Identify areas of inefficiency in your business, identify the network members and areas where there is lack of trust.

2. Continue Proof Of Concepts: For any new technology the general rule of thumb seems to 90:9:1 – 90% of organizations obtain basic information about the new technology, 9% try it as a Proof Of Concept, and 1% go on into production. For a technology like blockchain which is in its infancy, start small by choosing the right starter use case or segment of a bigger use case. It's a great way to get hands-on experience and become comfortable with the technology. Next, use an agile approach to iteratively expand your project as more resources become available. You can prioritize solution features across agile sprints to accelerate the development and deployment of a minimum viable product.

BIBLIOGRAPHY

Smith, A. (1776). *An Inquiry Into the Nature and Causes of the Wealth of Nations*.
An Inquiry Into the Nature and Causes of the Wealth of Nations v. 1. Strahan.

Roth, F. (2009). "The Effects of the Financial Crisis on Systemic Trust". In:

Christensen, C.M. (2015).
The Innovator's Dilemma: When New Technologies Cause Great Firms to Fail.
Harvard Business Review Press. ISBN: 9781633691797.

Pilkington, M. (2015). "Blockchain Technology: Principles and Applications". In:
URL: https://ssrn.com/abstract=2662660.

CITI (2016). *Digital Disruption*. URL: https://ir.citi.com/D%2F5GCKN6uoSvhbvCmUDS0
5SYsRaDvAykPjb5subGr7f1JMe8w2oX1bqpFm6RdjSRSpGzSaXhyXY%3D.

Government Office for Science (2016). *Distributed Ledger Technology: beyond blockchain*.
URL: https://assets.publishing.service.gov.uk/government/uploads/sy
stem/uploads/attachment_data/file/492972/gs-16-1-distributed-ledge
r-technology.pdf.

Hong King Monetary Authority (2016). *Whitepapr on Distributed Ledger Technology*.
URL: http://www.hkma.gov.hk/media/eng/doc/key-functions/finanical-i
nfrastructure/Whitepaper_On_Distributed_Ledger_Technology.pdf.

OutlierVentures (2017). *Community Token Economies*.

Friedlmaier, Maximilian, Andranik Tumasjan, and Isabell M. Welpe (2018).
Disrupting Industries With Blockchain.
URL: https://poseidon01.ssrn.com/delivery.php?ID=258105111101104113
123116001029108088038002035054002027096002014102001120002124086071
043103049011103001110086098025026117104089058017008015072081001097
065126025098022060049084091098116106069123126005106069010840.

Accenture (n.d.).
BLOCKCHAIN-ENABLED DISTRIBUTED LEDGERS: ARE INVESTMENT BANKS READY?
URL: https://www.accenture.com/ca-en/insight-blockchain-enabled-dis
tributed-ledgers-investment-banks.

Agenda, Digital Insurance (n.d.). *Everledger: blockchain-based diamond fraud detection.*
    URL: http://www.diabarcelona.com/es/everledger-blockchain-based-dia
    mond-fraud-detection/.

al, J. e. (n.d.). *The General Theory of Decentralized Applications, Dapps.*
    URL: https://github.com/DavidJohnstonCEO/DecentralizedApplications.

Allen, C. (n.d.). *Life with Alacrity.* URL: http://www.lifewithalacrity.com/2016/04/t
    he-path-to-self-soverereign-identity.html.

Allied Market Research (n.d.).
    Blockchain Distributed Ledger Market Expected to Reach $5,430 Million, Globally, by 2023.
    URL: https://www.alliedmarketresearch.com/press-release/blockchain
    -distributed-ledger-market.html.

American Banker (n.d.). *Banks pick IBM blockchain to expand digital ID project in Canada.*
    URL: https://www.americanbanker.com/news/canadian-banks-pick-ibm-bl
    ockchain-to-expand-digital-identity-project.

Anh Dinh, J. W.-L. (n.d.). *BLOCKBENCH: A Framework for Analyzing Private Blockchains.*
    URL: https://arxiv.org/pdf/1703.04057.pdf.

Atlantic, The (n.d.). *One Name to Rule Them All: Facebook's Identity Problem.* URL:
    https://www.theatlantic.com/technology/archive/2014/10/one-name-to
    -rule-them-all-facebook-still-insists-on-a-single-identity/381039/.

Back, A. (n.d.). *Hashcash - A Denial of Service Counter-Measure.*
    URL: http://hashcash.org/papers/hashcash.pdf.

Bank Innovation (n.d.). *Blockchain VC Investment Nears $500M in 2016.* URL: http://bankinn
    ovation.net/2017/03/blockchain-vc-investment-nears-500m-in-2016/.

Bevand, M. (n.d.). *Electricity consumption of Bitcoin: a market-based and technical analysis.*
    URL: http://blog.zorinaq.com/bitcoin-electricity-consumption/.

Bitcoin (n.d.). *Bitcoin.* URL: http://bitcoin.org.

BitcoinTalk (n.d.). *Bitcoin Forum.* URL: https://bitcointalk.org/index.php?topic=9
    1806.msg1012234#msg1012234.

Blockcerts (n.d.). *Blockcerts: The Open Initiative for Blockchain Certificates.*
    URL: http://www.blockcerts.org/guide/.

Blockchain.info (n.d.). *Block #170.* URL: https://blockchain.info/block/00000000d11
    45790a8694403d4063f323d499e655c83426834d4ce2f8dd4a2ee.

BlockchainTechnews (n.d.).
    BlockCypher and ShoCard partner on blockchain-based identity management.
    URL: https://www.blockchaintechnews.com/news/blockcypher-and-shocar
    d-partner-on-blockchain-based-identity-management/.

Brave New Coin (n.d.).
    Everledger Uses the Blockchain, Tackling Conflict Diamonds And Insurance Fraud.
    URL: https://bravenewcoin.com/news/everledger-uses-the-blockchain-t
    ackling-conflict-diamonds-and-insurance-fraud/.

Brown, R. G. (n.d.). *A SIMPLE MODEL FOR SMART CONTRACTS*. URL:
https://gendal.me/2015/02/10/a-simple-model-for-smart-contracts/.

Buterin, V. (n.d.[a]). *A NEXT GENERATION SMART CONTRACT & DECENTRALIZED
APPLICATION PLATFORM*. URL: https://www.weusecoins.com/assets/pdf/libr
ary/Ethereum_white_paper-a_next_generation_smart_contract_and_dece
ntralized_application_platform-vitalik-buterin.pdf.

— (n.d.[b]). *DAOs, DACs, DAs and More: An Incomplete Terminology Guide*.
URL: https://blog.ethereum.org/2014/05/06/daos-dacs-das-and-more-an
-incomplete-terminology-guide/.

Cann, O. (n.d.). *These are the top 10 emerging technologies of 2016*. URL: https://www.weforu
m.org/agenda/2016/06/top-10-emerging-technologies-2016.

Castor, A. (n.d.).
Gem Partners With Capital One for Blockchain-Based Health Care Claims Management.
Retrieved from BitcoinMagazine. URL:
https://bitcoinmagazine.com/articles/gem-partners-with-capital-one
-for-blockchain-based-health-care-claims-management-1477502028/.

Chainlink Research (n.d.). *Blockchain Gets Real*. URL: http://www.clresearch.com/resea
rch/detail.cfm?guid=A51F4BF5-3048-78A9-2FC4-30CEEE19CDC5.

ClearXchange (n.d.). *ECEIVE MONEY WHERE YOU ACTUALLY WANT IT – DIRECTLY IN YOUR
BANK ACCOUNT*. URL: https://www.clearxchange.com/.

Coindesk (n.d.[a]). *$11 Trillion Bet: DTCC to Process Derivatives With Blockchain Tech*.
URL: http://www.coindesk.com/11-trillion-bet-dtcc-clear-derivatives
-blockchain-tech/.

— (n.d.[b]). *$150 Million: Tim Draper-Backed Bancor Completes Largest-Ever ICO*.
URL: https://www.coindesk.com/150-million-tim-draper-backed-bancor
-completes-largest-ever-ico/.

— (n.d.[c]). *Circle Raises $50 Million With Goldman Sachs Support*. URL: http://www.coind
esk.com/circle-raises-50-million-with-goldman-sachs-support/.

— (n.d.[d]). *Everledger Brings Blockchain Tech to Fight Against Diamond Theft*. URL: http://w
ww.coindesk.com/everledger-blockchain-tech-fight-diamond-theft/.

— (n.d.[e]). *State of Blockchain Q4 2016*. URL:
https://www.slideshare.net/CoinDesk/state-of-blockchain-q4-2016.

— (n.d.[f]). *Understanding the DAO attack*.
URL: http://www.coindesk.com/understanding-dao-hack-journalists/.

Company, McKinsey & (n.d.). *Blockchain Technology in the Insurance Sector*.
URL: https://www.treasury.gov/initiatives/fio/Documents/McKinsey_FA
CI_Blockchain_in_Insurance.pdf.

Computerworld (n.d.).
How Walmart will use blockchain system to improve traceability of food supply.

URL: http://www.computerworlduk.com/iot/walmart-picks-ibm-bring-traceability-food-with-blockchain-3654841/.

CryptocoinsNews (n.d.).

Ethereum-Based Aragon Raises $25 Million Under 15 Minutes in Record ICO.

URL: https://www.cryptocoinsnews.com/ethereum-based-aragon-raises-25-million-15-minutes-record-ico/.

Cryptolization (n.d.). *Cryptocurrency market cap analysis.*

URL: https://cryptolization.com/.

CrytoCompare (n.d.). *The DAO, The Hack, The Soft Fork and The Hard Fork.*

URL: https://www.cryptocompare.com/coins/guides/the-dao-the-hack-the-soft-fork-and-the-hard-fork/.

dashlane (n.d.). *Online Overload – It's Worse Than You Thought.* URL: https://blog.dashlane.com/infographic-online-overload-its-worse-than-you-thought/.

Deloitte (n.d.[a]). *Blockchain & Cyber Securit.*

URL: https://www2.deloitte.com/content/dam/Deloitte/ie/Documents/Technology/IE%5CC%5CBlockchainandCyberPOV%5C0417.pdf.

— (n.d.[b]). *Blockchain: Trust economy.* URL: https://dupress.deloitte.com/dup-us-en/focus/tech-trends/2017/blockchain-trust-economy.html.

— (n.d.[c]). *Deloitte continues growing major blockchain initiative, teaming with five technology companies and announcing 20 prototypes in development.*

URL: https://www2.deloitte.com/mt/en/pages/about-deloitte/articles/mt-pr2016-008-deloitte-blockchain-initiative-with-five-tech-companies-and-20-prototypes-in-development.html.

DocuSign (n.d.). *DocuSign Showcases Smart Contracts & Payments Prototype Built for Visa's Connected Car Initiative.*

URL: https://www.docusign.com/press-releases/docusign-showcases-smart-contracts-payments-prototype-built-for-visas-connected-car.

Drake, N. (n.d.). *Help, I'm Trapped in Facebook's Absurd Pseudonym Purgatory.* URL: https://www.wired.com/2015/06/facebook-real-name-policy-problems/.

DTCC (n.d.). *DTCC Selects IBM, AXONI and R3 to Develop DTCC's Distributed Ledger Solution for Derivatives Processing.*

URL: http://www.dtcc.com/news/2017/january/09/dtcc-selects-ibm-axoni-and-r3-to-develop-dtccs-distributed-ledger-solution.

DuPont, Q. (n.d.). *Experiments in Algorithmic Governance: A history and ethnography of 'The DAO', a failed Decentralized Autonomous Organization.* URL: http://iqdupont.com/assets/documents/DUPONT-2017-Preprint-Algorithmic-Governance.pdf.

Economist (n.d.[a]). *The great chain of being sure about things.* URL: http://www.economist.com/news/briefing/21677228-technology-behind-bitcoin-lets-people-who-do-not-know-or-trust-each-other-build-dependable.

— (n.d.[b]). *Trust Machine.*
    URL: http://www.economist.com/news/leaders/21677198-technology-behi
    nd-bitcoin-could-transform-how-economy-works-trust-machine.

Ethereum (n.d.[a]). *Ethereum Network Status.* URL: https://ethstats.net/.

— (n.d.[b]). *Ethereum White Paper.*
    URL: https://github.com/ethereum/wiki/wiki/White-Paper#ethereum.

— (n.d.[c]). *The Ethereum Foundation.*
    URL: http://ethdocs.org/en/latest/introduction/foundation.html.

ETHNews (n.d.). *Walmart Tests Food Safety With Blockchain Traceability.*
    URL: https://www.ethnews.com/walmart-tests-food-safety-with-blockch
    ain-traceability.

Faster Payments (n.d.). *Faster Payments.* URL: http://www.fasterpayments.org.uk/.

FCA (n.d.). *Consumer warning about the risks of Initial Coin Offerings ('ICOs').*
    URL: https://www.fca.org.uk/news/statements/initial-coin-offerings
    ?lipi=urn%3Ali%3Apage%3Ad_flagship3_profile_view_base_recent_activ
    ity_details_all%3BQEn15UGtSwK5heoHt%2Bq2WA%3D%3D.

FICO (n.d.). *Options and Opportunities.*
    URL: http://subscribe.fico.com/millennialreport.

Flickr (n.d.). *Infographic The Paper Trail of a Shipping Container.* URL: https://www.flickr
    .com/photos/ibm%5C_media/33251213875/in/album-72157679386099830/.

Forbes (n.d.[a]). *Cryptocurrency ICOs Are Making Bitcoin Startups Richer than VCs Ever Did.*
    URL: http://fortune.com/2017/07/28/bitcoin-cryptocurrency-ico/.

— (n.d.[b]). *The SEC's Big Digital Coin Ruling: What It Means.*
    URL: http://fortune.com/2017/07/26/sec-icos/.

— (n.d.[c]). *Visa, Citi, Nasdaq Invest $30 Million In Blockchain Startup Chain.com.* URL:
    https://www.forbes.com/sites/laurashin/2015/09/09/visa-citi-nasdaq
    -invest-30-million-in-blockchain-startup-chain-com/#6a025d68199c.

forklog (n.d.). *Russia's Alpha Bank to Record Customer IDs on Blockchain.* URL: http://forklo
    g.net/russias-alpha-bank-to-record-customer-id-on-blockchain/.

Free Dictionary (n.d.). *Contract.*
    URL: http://legal-dictionary.thefreedictionary.com/contract.

Frost & Sullivan (n.d.). *Game Changers - Technologies Posted to Disrupt Industries.*
    URL: https://cds.frost.com/p/48979/#!/ppt/c?id=MAFB-01-00-00-00.

Futter, D. (n.d.).
    Blockchain Law: ICO Regulation and Other Legal Considerations in the Blockchain Ecosystem.
    URL: https://rimon.egnyte.com/dl/Pqvu8nrUSN.

Gawker (n.d.). *The Underground Website Where You Can Buy Any Drug Imaginable.*
    URL: http://gawker.com/the-underground-website-where-you-can-buy-an
    y-drug-imag-30818160.

GuardTime (n.d.). *Supply Chain Reimagined.* URL: http://www.guardtime.com.

Hackernoon (n.d.). *A Primer on Blockchains, Protocols, and Token Sales.*
    URL: https://hackernoon.com/a-primer-on-blockchains-protocols-and-t
    oken-sales-9ebe117b5759.

Harvard Business Review (n.d.[a]).
    Blockchain Will Help Us Prove Our Identities in a Digital World.
    URL: https://hbr.org/2017/03/blockchain-will-help-us-prove-our-iden
    tities-in-a-digital-world.

— (n.d.[b]). *The Truth About Blockchain.* URL: https://enterprisersproject.com/sit
    es/default/files/the_truth_about_blockchain.pdf.

Hess, Thomas (n.d.).
    Options for Formulating a Digital Transformation Strategy - MIS Quarterly Executive.
    URL: http://www.misqe.org/ojs2/execsummaries/MISQE_V15I2_Hessetal_W
    eb.pdf.

Holberston School (n.d.).
    Using the blockchain to secure and authentify Holberton School certificates.
    URL: https://blog.holbertonschool.com/using-the-blockchain-to-secur
    e-and-authentify-holberton-school-certificates/.

Hyperledger (n.d.[a]). *Hyperledger Fabric Documentation.*
    URL: http://hyperledger-fabric.readthedocs.io/en/latest/ledger.html.

— (n.d.[b]). *Hyperledger Overview.*
    URL: https://docs.google.com/presentation/d/1lM_FS1TDDN-5yjL3lM61hW
    _PIFAvGA592XN-Sv_5LrU/edit#slide=id.g22bf4fd136_0_0.

IBM (n.d.[a]). URL: http://www-03.ibm.com/press/us/en/photo/51717.ws.

— (n.d.[b]). *Blockchain basics.* URL: https://console.bluemix.net/docs/services
    /blockchain/ibmblockchain%5Coverview.html.

— (n.d.[c]). *Blockchain rewires financial markets.* URL: https://www-01.ibm.com/common
    /ssi/cgi-bin/ssialias?htmlfid=GBP03469USEN&.

— (n.d.[d]). *Business integration architecture and patterns.*
    URL: https://www.ibm.com/support/knowledgecenter/en/SSQH9M%5C7.0.0
    /com.ibm.websphere.wps.doc/doc/cdev%5Cpgarchpat.html.

— (n.d.[e]). *Empowering the edge.*
    URL: https://www-935.ibm.com/services/multimedia/GBE03662USEN.pdf.

— (n.d.[f]). *Forward Together.*
    URL: https://www-935.ibm.com/services/studies/csuite/.

— (n.d.[g]). *IBM and SecureKey Technologies to Deliver Blockchain-Based Digital Identity
    Network for Consumers.*
    URL: http://www-03.ibm.com/press/us/en/pressrelease/51841.wss.

— (n.d.[h]).
    IBM Global Financing uses blockchain technology to quickly resolve financial disputes.
    URL: https://www.ibm.com/blockchain/infographic/finance.html.

— (n.d.[i]). *IBM IGF Blockchain.*
 URL: https://www.ibm.com/blockchain/infographic/finance.html.
— (n.d.[j]). *IGF Blockchain.*
 URL: https://www.ibm.com/blockchain/infographic/finance.html.
— (n.d.[k]). *TenneT unlocks distributed flexibility via IBM Blockchain.*
 URL: https://www-03.ibm.com/press/us/en/pressrelease/52243.wss.
— (n.d.[l]). *The Economy of Things: Extracting new value from the Internet of Things.*
 URL: https://www-01.ibm.com/common/ssi/cgi-bin/ssialias?subtype=XB
 &infotype=PM&htmlfid=GBE03678USEN&attachment=GBE03678USEN.PDF.
Inbound Marketing Blog (n.d.).
 6 Important Stats on How Consumer Behavior Has Changed in the Digital Age.
 URL: http://www.inboundmarketingagents.com/inbound-marketing-agents
 -blog/6-important-stats-on-how-consumer-behavior-has-changed-in-th
 e-digital-age.
Innovate Finance (n.d.). *The 2016 VC FinTech Investment Landscape by Innovate Finance.*
 URL: https://www.slideshare.net/innovatefinance/the-2016-vc-fintech
 -investment-landscape-71849828/1.
Jagers, C. (n.d.). *Digital Identity and the Blockchain.* URL: https://medium.com/learning
 -machine-blog/digital-identity-and-the-blockchain-10de0e7d7734.
Janrain (n.d.). *Online Americans Fatigued by Password Overload Janrain Study Finds.*
 URL: http://janrain.com/about/newsroom/press-releases/online-americ
 ans-fatigued-by-password-overload-janrain-study-finds.
Jentzsch, C. (n.d.).
 Decentralized Autonomous Organization to Automate Governance Final Draft - Under Review.
 URL: https://download.slock.it/public/DAO/WhitePaper.pdf.
Ken Jordan, J. H. (n.d.). *The Augmented Social Network.* URL:
 http://asn.planetwork.net/asn-archive/AugmentedSocialNetwork.pdf.
Konst, S. (n.d.). *Sichere Log-Dateien auf Grundlage kryptographisch verketteter Einträge.*
 URL: http://www.konst.de/stefan/seclog.pdf.
KPMG (n.d.). *Consensus - Immutable agreement for Internet of value.*
 URL: https://assets.kpmg.com/content/dam/kpmg/pdf/2016/06/kpmg-bloc
 kchain-consensus-mechanism.pdf.
Krishna, A. (n.d.). *Blockchain and the Future of Trust.*
 URL: https://www.ibm.com/blogs/think/2016/06/blockchain-trust/.
Lehdonvirta, V. (n.d.). *The blockchain paradox: Why distributed ledger technologies may do little
 to transform the economy.* URL:
 http://blogs.oii.ox.ac.uk/policy/the-blockchain-paradox-why-distri
 buted-ledger-technologies-may-do-little-to-transform-the-economy/.

Lui, S. (n.d.). *THE DEMOGRAPHICS OF BITCOIN (PART 1 UPDATED).*
URL: https://web.archive.org/web/20130629065001/http://simulacrum.c
c:80/2013/03/04/the-demographics-of-bitcoin-part-1-updated/.

Mann, Steve (n.d.). *Declaration of Veillance.*
URL: http://wearcam.org/declaration.pdf.

Marketing Land (n.d.).
Report: E-commerce accounted for 11.7% of total retail sales in 2016, up 15.6% over 2015.
URL: http://marketingland.com/report-e-commerce-accounted-11-7-tota
l-retail-sales-2016-15-6-2015-207088.

Markets and Markets (n.d.[a]). *Blockchain Market by Provider, Application (Payments, Exchanges,
Smart Contracts, Documentation, Digital Identity, Clearing and Settlement), Organization
Size, Vertical, and Region - Global Forecast to 2021.* URL: http://www.marketsandmarke
ts.com/Market-Reports/blockchain-technology-market-90100890.html.

— (n.d.[b]). *Blockchain Technology Market - Global Forecast to 2021.*

Mashable (n.d.). *This Android malware is hacking into your Google account to install apps.*
URL: http://mashable.com/2016/11/30/android-google-gooligan-hack/%5
C#.UZ7.1Gpjmqb.

Mattila, J. (n.d.). *THE BLOCKCHAIN PHENOMENON.* URL: http://www.brie.berkeley.ed
u/wp-content/uploads/2015/02/Juri-Mattila-.pdf.

McKinsey (n.d.). *How blockchains could change the world.*
URL: http://www.mckinsey.com/industries/high-tech/our-insights/how
-blockchains-could-change-the-world.

McKinsey & Company (n.d.). *Beyond the hype: Blockchains in capital markets.*
URL: https://www.mckinsey.com/netherlands/our-insights/beyond-the-h
ype-blockchains-in-capital-markets.

Medium (n.d.). *Blockchain technology: Redefining trust for a global, digital economy.*
URL: https://medium.com/mit-media-lab-digital-currency-initiative/b
lockchain-technology-redefining-trust-for-a-global-digital-economy
-1dc869593308.

Merkle, The (n.d.). *What is Segregated Witness.*
URL: https://themerkle.com/what-is-segregated-witness/.

Mery, S. (n.d.). *Make your blockchain smart contracts smarter with business rules.*
URL: https://www.ibm.com/developerworks/library/mw-1708-mery-blockc
hain/1708-mery.html.

Microsoft (n.d.). *A Large Scale Study of Web Password Habits.*
URL: https://www.microsoft.com/en-us/research/publication/a-large-s
cale-study-of-web-password-habits/.

Microsoft Azure (n.d.). *What does identity mean in today's physical and digital world?*
URL: https://azure.microsoft.com/en-us/blog/what-does-identity-mean
-in-today-s-physical-and-digital-world/.

Mik, D. (n.d.). *Smart Contracts: Terminology, Technical Limitations and Real World Complexity.*
URL: https://papers.ssrn.com/sol3/papers.cfm?abstract_id=3038406.

Miller, M. (n.d.). *The Digital Path:Smart Contracts and the Third World.*
URL: http://www.erights.org/talks/pisa/paper/index.html.

Mills, Sarah Bake (n.d.). *Blockchain Design Principle.* URL: https://medium.com/design-i
bm/blockchain-design-principles-599c5c067b6e.

Ministry of Industry and Information Technology of People's Republic of China (n.d.).
URL: http://www.miit.gov.cn/n1146290/n4388791/c5781140/content.html.

MIT Sloan School of Management (n.d.). *Some Simple Economics of the Blockchain.*
URL: https://papers.ssrn.com/sol3/papers.cfm?abstract_id=2874598.

Moodys (n.d.[a]). URL: http://www.moodys.com/researchdocumentcontentpage.asp
x?docid=PBC_1023913.

— (n.d.[b]).
Robust, Cost-effective Applications Key to Unlocking Blockchain's Potential Credit Benefits.
URL: http://www.moodys.com/researchdocumentcontentpage.aspx?docid=P
BC_1023913.

Nakamoto, S. (n.d.). *Bitcoin: A Peer-to-Peer Electronic Cash System.*
URL: http://nakamotoinstitute.org/bitcoin/.

OpenID (n.d.). *What is OpenID.* URL: http://openid.net/what-is-openid/.

Peertracks (n.d.). *A new foundation for the Music World.* URL: http://peertracks.com/.

People Are Making Their Own Ethereum Rigs To Mine Cryptocurrency (n.d.).
Retrieved from ibtimes.com. URL: http://www.ibtimes.com/ethereum-news-peop
le-are-making-their-own-ethereum-rigs-mine-cryptocurrency-2552653.

Pew Research Center (n.d.). *News Use Across Social Media Platform 2016.*
URL: http://www.journalism.org/2016/05/26/news-use-across-social-me
dia-platforms-2016/.

Ponemon Institute (n.d.). *The true cost of compliance.* URL: http://www.ponemon.org/loca
l/upload/file/True_Cost_of_Compliance_Report_copy.pdf.

PYMNTS (n.d.). *NYSE, USAA and BBVA Make $75M Coinbase Investment.*
URL: http://www.pymnts.com/news/2015/nyse-usaa-and-bbva-make-75m-co
inbase-investment/.

Rauchs, D. G. (n.d.). *GLOBAL CRYPTOCURRENCY BENCHMARKING STUDY.*
URL: https://www.jbs.cam.ac.uk/fileadmin/user_upload/research/centr
es/alternative-finance/downloads/2017-04-20-global-cryptocurrency
-benchmarking-study.pdf.

Richardson, Chris (n.d.). *Pattern: API Gateway / Backend for Front-End.*
URL: http://microservices.io/patterns/apigateway.html.

Ripple (n.d.[a]). *Ripple Adds Several New Banks to Global Network.* URL: https://ripple.co
m/ripple_press/ripple-adds-several-new-banks-global-network/.

— (n.d.[b]). *Website.* URL: http://www.ripple.com.

ScienceDaily (n.d.).
> *Big Data, for better or worse: 90% of world's data generated over last two years.*
> URL: https://www.sciencedaily.com/releases/2013/05/130522085217.htm.

Securities and Exchange Commission (n.d.). *SECURITIES EXCHANGE ACT OF 1934.*
> URL: https://www.sec.gov/litigation/investreport/34-81207.pdf.

SecurityGladiators (n.d.). *How Much Energy Does Bitcoin Use? A Lot It Turns Out.*
> URL: https://securitygladiators.com/bitcoin-uses-energy-a-lot/.

Stark, J. (n.d.). *Making Sense of Blockchain Smart Contracts.*
> URL: http://www.coindesk.com/making-sense-smart-contracts/.

Surden, H. (n.d.). *Computable Contracts.* URL: https://lawreview.law.ucdavis.edu/is
sues/46/2/articles/46-2_surden.pdf.

Szabo, N. (n.d.). *Formalizing and Securing Relationships on Public Networks.*
> URL: http://ojphi.org/ojs/index.php/fm/article/view/548.

TechCrunch (n.d.).
> *Former Mozilla CEO raises $35M in under 30 seconds for his browser startup Brave.*
> URL: https://techcrunch.com/2017/06/01/brave-ico-35-million-30-seco
> nds-brendan-eich/.

Techopedia (n.d.). *Digital Identity.*
> URL: https://www.techopedia.com/definition/23915/digital-identity.

Telegraph, The (n.d.). *Mobile web usage overtakes desktop for first time.*
> URL: http://www.telegraph.co.uk/technology/2016/11/01/mobile-web-us
> age-overtakes-desktop-for-first-time/.

The Hacker News (n.d.). *Over 1 Million Google Accounts Hacked by 'Gooligan' Android Malware.*
> URL: http://thehackernews.com/2016/11/hack-google-account.html.

The New York Times (n.d.). *Barred From Facebook, and Wondering Why.*
> URL: https://www.nytimes.com/2014/09/20/your-money/kicked-off-faceb
> ook-and-wondering-why.html?%5C_r=0.

The World Bank (n.d.). *The Identity Target in the Post-2015 Development Agenda.*
> URL: http://www.worldbank.org/en/topic/ict/brief/the-identity-targe
> t-in-the-post-2015-development-agenda-connections-note-19.

Time (n.d.). *Almost Nobody Trusts Financial Institutions.* URL:
> http://time.com/money/4293845/trust-financial-institutions-study/.

Unknown (n.d.). *Blockchain Technology Market Analysis By Type (Public, Private, And Hybrid),*
> *By Application (Financial Services, Consumer/Industrial Products, Technology, Media &*
> *Telecom, Healthcare, Transportation, And Public Sector), By Region, & Segment Forecasts.*
> URL: http://www.grandviewresearch.com/industry-analysis/blockchain
> -technology-market.

uPort (n.d.). *UPORT: A PLATFORM FOR SELF-SOVEREIGN IDENTITY.* URL: https://whitepa
per.uport.me/uPort%5Cwhitepaper%5CDRAFT20170221.pdf.

US Securities and Exchange Commission (n.d.).

SEC Issues Investigative Report Concluding DAO Tokens, a Digital Asset, Were Securities.

URL: https://www.sec.gov/news/press-release/2017-131.

Viet, Daniel (n.d.). *Business Models - An Information Systems Research Agenda.*

URL: http://www.wiwi.uni-augsburg.de/de/bwl/veit/lehre/downloads/bm_bise_paper.pdf.

Wikipedia (n.d.[a]). *Bit Gold proposal.*

URL: https://en.bitcoin.it/wiki/Bit_Gold_proposal.

— (n.d.[b]). *Code of Hammurabi.*

URL: https://en.wikipedia.org/wiki/Code_of_Hammurabi.

— (n.d.[c]). *Code of Hammurabi.*

URL: https://en.wikipedia.org/wiki/Code_of_Hammurabi.

— (n.d.[d]). *Restatement (Second) of Contracts.* URL:

https://en.wikipedia.org/wiki/Restatement_(Second)_of_Contracts.

— (n.d.[e]). *Single Euro Payments Area.*

URL: https://en.wikipedia.org/wiki/Single_Euro_Payments_Area.

— (n.d.[f]). *The DAO.*

URL: https://en.wikipedia.org/wiki/The%5CDAO%5C(organization).

— (n.d.[g]). *Uniform Commercial Code.*

URL: https://en.wikipedia.org/wiki/Uniform_Commercial_Code.

Wired (n.d.). *Block Chain 2.0: The Renaissance of Money.*

URL: https://www.wired.com/insights/2015/01/block-chain-2-0/.

World Economic Forum (n.d.[a]). *Realizing the Potential of Blockchain.* URL: http://www3.weforum.org/docs/WEF_Realizing_Potential_Blockchain.pdf.

— (n.d.[b]). *The future of financial infrastructure.* URL: http://www3.weforum.org/docs/WEF_The_future_of_financial_infrastructure.pdf.

WSJ (n.d.). *Cryptocurrency a Response to Financial Crisis.*

URL: http://www.wsj.com/video/cryptocurrency-a-response-to-financial-crisis-says-ceo/D28A8012-413F-447E-AA5A-F1911BA64FC3.html.

Yelowitz, Aaron (n.d.). *Characteristics of Bitcoin users: an analysis of Google search data.*

URL: http://yelowitz.com/Wilson_Yelowitz_Bitcoin.pdf.

GLOSSARY

ADEPT	Autonomous Decentralized Peer-to-Peer Telemetry
BaaS	Blockchain-as-a-Service
CAGR	Compound Annual Growth Rate
CCICADA	Command Control and Interoperability Center for Advanced Data Analytics
CDC	Center for Disease Control
DAH	Digital Asset Holdings
DAO	Digital Autonomous Organization
DApps	Distributed Applications *or* Decentralized Applications
DDBMS	Distributed Database Management System
DIACC	Digital ID and Authentication Council of Canada
DLT	Distributed Ledger Technology
DTCC	Depository Trust and Clearing Corporation
EEA	Ethereum Enterprise Alliance
EDI	Electronic Data Interchange
EVM	Ethereum Virtual Machine
FCAPS	Fauly, Configuration, Accounting, Performance, Security
FICO	Fair, Isaac and Company

FINMA	Swiss Financial Market Supervisory Authority
Fintech	Financial Technology
GDPR	General Data Protection Regulation
HAACP	Hazard Analysis Critical Control Point
HSM	Harware Security Module
ICO	Initial Coin Offering
ITO	Initial Token Offering
IGF	IBM Global Financing
IoT	Internet of Things
IPFS	InterPlanetary File System
KYC	Know Your Customer
MHFG	Mizuho Financial Group
MQTT	Message Queuing Telemetry Transport
MRI	Magnetic Resonance Imaging
MSP	Member Service Provider
NAB	National Australia Bank
NASAA	North American Securities Administrators Association
ODM	Operational Decision Manager
PBFT	Practical Byzantine Fault Tolerance
PII	Personally Identifiable Information
PKI	Public Key Interchange
PoC	Proof of Concept
PoET	Proof of Elapsed Time
PoS	Proof of State
PoW	Proof of Work
QoQ	Quarter on Quarter
REST	Representational State Transfer

ROI	Return on Investment
SCB	Siam Commercial Bank
SDK	Software Development Kit
SEPA	Single Euro Payments Area
SOR	Systems of Record
TIW	Trade Information Warehouse
WEF	World Economic Forum

INDEX